This book is dedicated to the fine people
of St. Paul-Reformation Lutheran Church
and Wingspan Ministry in Saint Paul, Minnesota.

Quite beyond providing the financial assistance
to make this book a reality,
the manner of our life together,
passionately seeking to do justice,
to show compassion,
and to walk humbly with God and one another,
fills me with hope.
Within our walls
the tune of a welcoming God
is always in the air.

"We have heard that God is with you,
and so we wish to share in your destiny."
Zechariah 8:23

Contents

Hymns

Foreword

Word weaver. Dreamer. Poet. Theologian. Husband. Father. Friend. Ally.

We are richer for sensing through his writings the spiritual graces God has bestowed on David Weiss. He is a unique ally of gay, lesbian, bisexual, and transgender (GLBT) people and all who have felt God's presence in their sexuality. His first book includes essays, poetry, and song lyrics, all of which surprise us into seeing the immediacy of God in the present.

I met David shortly before the extraordinary service of ordination I experienced in 2001 along with 1,100 people from across the country who gathered with members of St. Paul-Reformation Lutheran Church. One week later he organized three vans loaded with students from Luther College in Iowa to be present in song and support when our congregation was picketed by a conservative congregation from Kansas. On that day, David facilitated lyrical reflections of young voices that filled sacred space with song, helping a community stand fast in the face of garish caricature and harmful signs and words.

David and his wife, Margaret Schuster, were the first opposite-gender couple to seek my counsel as they contemplated marriage. Theirs was the first legal marriage I officiated after my ordination papers were filed with the county and state. I consider them special allies in my life and spiritual journey, having shared important moments of ecclesiastical disobedience flowing from a mutual embrace of incarnational theology.

David's essays engage us in the theological debates and pedagogical efforts of more than a decade, as he wrestles in context with the church, beliefs about God, humanity, and sexual orientations. One of the strong characteristics of his writing is his ability to assist his audience to see through the strength of his self-location as an ally of GLBT people.

In his Personal Word of Testimony (1994) David said: "God is fully capable of preaching good news through the voices of gay and lesbian people." In speaking this truth, he came to know firsthand that "Coming out, even as an ally, has its price." David has learned and relearned the lessons of coming

1

out, just as GLBT people do across the span of our lives. David holds a keen appreciation for the graces he has experienced with GLBT friends and colleagues.

David's writing affirms the Lutheran perspective that God's Word is living and dynamic. Jesus Christ is incarnate Word. Scripture is written Word. Proclamation is spoken Word. When his lyric tunes are sung, his poems and prose read, we are invited to recognize again the dynamic presence of God in our midst. David takes seriously his role as a member of the Body of Christ. His theology immerses us in body theology.

In this volume, *To the Tune of a Welcoming God*, we experience the graceful force of an ally preaching good news. David's theology of welcome, hospitality, and openness to the Spirit's guidance each inform his theological writings. He moves us along paths of continuing reformation.

David's lyrics bring new images to sometimes ancient tunes, infusing contemporary meaning in the melodies of the church's psyche. His words can be shockingly beautiful.

We hope this book will expand David's audience, for he is called to write and his is a voice that needs be heard across the ecumenical spectrum as denominations continue to wrestle with the place of GLBT persons in church and society. The Wingspan Ministry of St. Paul-Reformation is pleased to partner with David to put this book before the public.

The Rev. Anita C. Hill
Saint Paul, Minnesota
April 29, 2008

By way of introduction. . .

For the better part of a decade now I have been wrestling with and writing about the place of gay, lesbian, bisexual, and transgender persons in the love of God and the life of the Lutheran church. I will let the essays and hymns collected here speak for themselves on that count. Yet I have increasingly come to see this issue as fundamentally a challenge for *straight* Christians to come to closer terms with their own sexuality. Most of the essays have been authored in response to specific situations, and in them I focus most often on sexuality at the margins; but I sincerely hope that my thoughts promote more reflection as well among those of us whose own sexuality is less marginal but often just as unfamiliar to us.

I write as a theologian and poet, a person trained to think about God with discipline, and a person driven to imagine God with vivid words and unexpected images.

I have arranged the essays, with only a few exceptions, in the order I authored them. And I have left them largely in the form they first appeared. I don't consider them in any way limited to that original context, but theology never comes from nowhere, so it feels appropriate to let these essays speak from the places they were born. Because I write out of my experience in the Evangelical Lutheran Church in America (ELCA), I sometimes address events that are specifically Lutheran, but I suspect even those essays will resonate with many in other denominational settings. And, because this is a collection of essays, some themes will reappear and evolve over these pages. That, too, is how theology happens. And I am content to let that be seen as well.

I could acknowledge more persons than any reader would have patience to read, so I will content myself to name just these few. First, my parents, Carol and Frederick Weiss. From my childhood they showed me that the practice of faith is the practice of hospitality. Hardly free from the prejudices about sexuality that infected virtually every Christian three and four decades ago, they nevertheless introduced me unfailingly to the Welcoming God long before any of us could imagine the wideness of that welcome. Also, the 90 or so students at Luther College who accompanied me for three years in a dar-

3

ing experiment reading "Gay, Lesbian, Bisexual, and Transgender Voices in Theology" together. The challenge and privilege of teaching that class is one of the defining moments in my life. And finally, my wife, Margaret. If I write of the married mystery of sexuality and spirituality with passion, conviction, and tenderness, it is because of her. What I first imagined, I discovered with Margaret—and in our love I have discovered yet far more than I could have imagined on my own.

I hope these essays bring you understanding and insight. Most of all, I hope they sow the seeds of compassion throughout the church. And I pray for the day to come soon when the harvest is ripe and abundant.

David Robert Weiss
1359 Blair Avenue
Saint Paul, Minnesota 55104

This poem/creed describes the faith out of which my writing flows. Although it does not speak directly to the issue of welcome for GLBT persons in the church, the tune of such welcome can clearly be heard. My companionship with and advocacy for GLBT persons is an expression of this faith.

1. Credo
(April 2001)

I believe in God,
the Great Mystery that is the Source of all that is.
I believe that God is beyond our words
and surely beyond our genders,
but that we are still invited to name God as best we can,
with humility and wonder.
I believe in God's love for all creation, not just humanity.
I believe in God's yearning
that justice hold sway in every corner of creation
and in God's anxious longing
for Sabbath joy to fill the cosmos.
I believe that the deep beauty of Jesus' life
is a true revelation of God's desire to see compassion
at the center of human community.
I believe that Jesus' healings, parables, and table fellowship
reveal the truth of God active in our midst.
And I believe that in Jesus' life
we hear an invitation to echo such compassion
in our own lives.
I believe that Jesus' death
reminds us that oppressive power
will stop at nothing—
then or now—to silence compassion.
And I believe that resurrection
names the miracle that takes place—
then and now—whenever we rededicate
our lives to compassion
thereby announcing that even death
cannot silence the love of God.

I believe that besides Jesus' life
and besides the biblical text,
other lives and other texts also bear the truth of God—
and that our lives are richer for listening well
to the movement of God in many places.
I believe that God continues to be present still today
and that the Holy Breath of God blows
whenever and wherever compassion is born,
whether in our words, deeds, or rituals.
I believe we have a special responsibility
to gather in community and share rituals,
both ancient and fresh,
that exercise our imaginations,
both bodily and spiritually
for the practice of compassion.
I believe that in our lives
we have the capacity to move God,
this loving mystery that dwells at the heart of all that is,
to the point of tears.
And I commit myself,
with my brothers and sisters and the whole of creation,
to living in ways that seek to move God to tears of joy.
Amen.

This is a short statement I shared with the members of Christ the King Lutheran Church in South Bend, Indiana during our discussion of the ELCA's first attempt at a Sexuality Statement in 1994. Offered with a shaking voice, this was my first public moment of advocacy.

2. A Personal Word of Testimony Offered to Christ the King Lutheran
(1994)

The [ELCA] study document lists as its sources Scripture, empirical understanding of sexual orientation, and the witness of gay and lesbian Christians, yet it fails to mention in any substantial manner at all the third source. The statement summarizes current empirical understanding of sexual orientation and reviews biblical scholarship on relevant passages, demonstrating how these work to form and justify its own position. But, though the statement exhorts us to listen to gays and lesbians as part of the same process, *it stops short of telling us what they have to say*, and how their particular input has shaped the present draft. Their testimony deserves an explicit hearing not simply in response to the statement but in its very making. I have no doubt that the gay and lesbian person on the Task Force, as well as the articulate witness of many Christian homosexual writers, were influential in the drafting of the document. *My point is more that the statement does not specifically tell us what particular warrants and wisdom have been brought to this discussion by the committed involvement of gay and lesbian Christians. And we are poorer for not sensing more concretely the power of their spiritual perseverance and the unique graces which God has bestowed upon them.*

I am not homosexual, nor am I aware of anyone in my immediate family who is, but I have known enough gay and lesbian persons, and I have known them well enough, to feel the need to speak a word of testimony on their behalf.

As an adolescent, hungry for a feeling of God's presence that seemed utterly denied to me, it was a gay man, a former Sunday School teacher of mine, who was able to speak to me in words that rang true, in words that were gospel to me. He said that God always comes to us, sometimes later rather than sooner, sometimes with more difficulty than ease, but that God always comes. He could speak with an authenticity that gave me hope because as a gay man denied his proper vocation in ordained ministry, he knew all too well the lateness and the difficulty with which God sometimes comes.

During my three years as a seminary student, I wrestled deeply with my own sense of vocation. As I struggled to discern where God was leading me, among the handful of close friends who helped me follow more faithfully, were three fellow seminarians. All were homosexual, and all were keenly aware of the awesome mystery of hearing the call of God, and of not being sure of how or whether to answer it. Precisely because they shared with me a commitment to discerning their own Christian vocations, and what that meant for them at the very core of their being, there was good news in our words to one another.

Finally, I lived with a gay man for a year before I was married. He didn't minister to me in any crucial way, like the others I've mentioned. But he did minister, in significant ways of service and friendship, to just about everyone around him, at work, at church, and at play. I say humbly that he remains probably the most saintly person I have known in my life, and all the more saintly because he would be both surprised and embarrassed to hear me say that. My life is richer, my own sense of calling much more humble, for simply having shared a small mobile home with this quietly holy man.

There have certainly been many heterosexual friends who have ministered to and befriended me as well over the years, and for them I am equally grateful. But my point is that time and again I have learned that God is fully capable of preaching good news through the voices and lives of gay and lesbian people. Their sexuality doesn't prevent them from doing ministry, whether as ordained pastors or as lay people. If anything, *because* of their sexual orientation they have a special kinship with Christ, beyond those of us heterosexuals, who, like birds, have nests, or, like foxes, have dens. They don't—at least not if we can help it, it seems.

Because genuine affirmation is so rare for them, they have a keen appreciation for grace that we heterosexuals too easily take for granted. For most of us, to hear that God has claimed us in love, however awesome and comforting we may find that, it is still by and large a word which society at least doesn't go out of its way to deny to us. But for homosexuals, to be claimed by God is to hear Hosea's words—really to live his words—in a way we can only faintly remember most of the time, when Hosea (2:23) declares on behalf of God, "And I will have pity on Not pitied, and I will say to Not my people, 'You are my people'; and they shall answer, 'Thou art my God'."

For the gay and lesbian people whom I have known, grace has been too real, good news has been far too abundant in their lives for me to believe anything other than that their orientations are a gift from God; and not simply a gift to themselves, but a gift through which they can serve the Church. *We only fail to discern an essential facet of the Body of Christ* (I Corinthians 11:29) *when we fail to recognize the sign of the cross in their lives next to our own.*

This essay, along with the one following it, is a good introduction to my journey. Here I refer to the piece that follows as my entry into advocacy. Certainly the statement at Christ the King came first by several years, but the "Words offered" essay has always felt like a more significant doorway. Perhaps because the Christ the King statement was shared with a roomful of persons that I could see and whom I knew, while the "Words offered" essay appeared in a student newspaper with a circulation of 10,000 and set my ideas out for an entire campus community to see—and react to. Anyway, while teaching at Luther College, I was asked to share some thoughts on "Spirituality and Coming Out" as part of Luther's Coming Out Day recognition. This presented a bit of a challenge for me as I am an ally, not an out GLBT person. However, I knew that even on Luther's relatively friendly campus, the price paid for being both out and Christian could be quite high. So this is a short reflection I offered on my "coming out" as an ally for GLBT persons.

3. Spirituality and Coming Out
(October 1999)

I "came out" in February 1997. By then I had already come to a fairly well-developed sense of why I affirmed the integrity of sexual orientations other than just heterosexuality. Driven by more than simply tolerance, I was increasingly persuaded that God's freedom to love, affirm, and include such persons was far bigger than any of the prejudices I grew up with. I had a number of gay and lesbian friends, and I was openly, even articulately supportive of them—behind closed doors. Not that I was in any way anti-gay in public. I was just decidedly *silent*.

While a graduate student at Notre Dame I read through the regular waves of debate over homosexuality in the daily student newspaper (debates carried out almost entirely by straight persons). I was disturbed by the rhetoric, but remained otherwise quiet. Notre Dame's Catholic tradition wasn't my own. This was not my issue. Not my cause. Bottom line: not my life, so why take the risk?

In the spring of 1996 I began teaching at Notre Dame, and very subtly my perspective began to change. The mass of Notre Dame undergraduates, previously just a sea of faces to me, suddenly and inescapably had names . . . feelings . . . and lives. Then, the following February I read a poem in *Scholastic*, a weekly student magazine, entitled "Living in Fear." It was written by an anonymous gay senior student at Notre Dame and recounted his daily four-year battle toward self-acceptance while driven by fear to remain in the closet. This time, perhaps because this wasn't a debate but a poignant lament, I wasn't "disturbed but quiet"; instead, I found myself weeping and raging. Late into the night I poured myself out in a long letter of response that I titled, "Words offered at the end of the day to an unknown friend living in fear." In it I ransacked the Bible for every manner of image to comfort and affirm him (and there are many of these!). As I put it in the letter, "I see now that if God keeps silent in the face of your anguish, it is only because I wouldn't lend God the use of my words." Later on I wrote, "Against all this [the fear] that you know so well I can offer only words—but maybe this is precisely what I have not done often enough or loud enough or long enough."

When my letter ran in the next week's *Scholastic*, I was "out." An ally. And there was no going back. I received a good number of e-mails of gratitude—but also more than a few words of derision. Coming out—even just as an ally—has its price. But it also has its rewards, which leads me to my point about coming out and spirituality. I had reached a place where, for me *not* to come out publicly as an ally of GLBT persons would have been, by my silence, to deny the very graciousness of the God who has encountered me. Instead, coming out as an ally has afforded me the chance to get on with the essential work of integrating my personal spirituality with my public commitments—the vocation of living my whole life in response to God's grace. I know from friends that this is true for GLBT persons as well. It's hard to hear the gospel in private if fear keeps you in the closet in public.

So I might be tempted to close with an invitation to all GLBT persons to "come out," but I don't think that's my invitation to make, at least not directly. I *can* say, if you're an ally still in the closet, National Coming Out Day is for you, too. However, my direct task is to keep on "coming out" myself as an ally, again and again, to do what I can to make the room beyond the closet a place that is safe when the closet door is opened by someone from the inside. And that's not something I do as an "extra" or "add-on" to my spirituality; it's the way I bear witness to the God I know.

11

This prose-poem first appeared in a February 1997 issue of Scholastic magazine at the University of Notre Dame. To this day, I do not know the identity of this "unknown friend."

4. Words Offered at the End of the Day to an Unknown Friend Living in Fear
(February 2, 1997)

I need to say this quietly in deference to your eloquent anguish. But I need to say it nonetheless. And I am angry, and it will be hard to keep my voice down; angry not *at* you but *for* you. And if I misread the last lines of your poem and you already know all this, that's okay. I'm sure someone else needs to hear it.

You say, "God knows, but God loves me anyway." Wait. Let me say it gently but firmly—unequivocally. God does *not* love you "anyway"—*despite* your being gay. God does not need to overlook the way you are to smile at the beauty of your humanity, at the earthy reflection of divine love as you are gaily—and I don't mean just "happily"—*imago Dei.*

Do you hear me, my friend? I will be downright strident about this because I see now that if God keeps silent in the face of your anguish, it is only because I wouldn't lend God the use of my words. Well, here they are.

When Hosea spoke of a day when God would have pity on "Not-pitied" and would say to "Not-my-people," you *are* my people—Hosea meant *you,* and I hope that day is *now.* When Isaiah welcomed foreigners and eunuchs (ever before outcast from the presence of God) into the Temple—well, Isaiah meant to welcome *you* as well, and to name your praise, like their praise, as *more* dear to God than even that of the faithful Jews (or Christians), perhaps because your praise is brought over the objections and insults of so many of us—and yet still finds its way to God. And when Peter was treated to that heavenly picnic of assorted forbidden foods, it was to remind him of Isaiah's self-same insight, that the church dare not exclude those who come at God's own call.

When Jesus stopped to speak and sip with the Samaritan woman at the well, perhaps she, too, thought that his fellowship came to her "anyway," *despite* her ethnic outcast baggage. But I tell you, my friend, and I am not scared to be flamboyant if need be: Jesus offered her living words and living water *because* of who she was. He relished her Samaritan beauty. He chose her for the Kingdom, and when he did, he meant for *you* to feel chosen, too, not *despite* but *because* of your gayness. So, when you picture her and him standing at the well, remember that while many in the church might prefer you didn't exist, or at least didn't tell us who you are, Jesus is stopping to chat because you caught his eye not "anyway"—but *just the way* you are.

Can you hear me, yet, my friend? I am not afraid to be audacious if I have to. When Jesus sent his disciples out two by two, he said to them if any town refused to welcome them in his name, well, on Judgment Day those towns would fare far worse than Sodom and Gomorrah. Okay, it isn't in the text—I admit it—but I will say it anyway because it's true: Jesus meant to say as much to all you same-sex couples who, not unlike those disciples, come, two by two, hoping for a bit of hospitality from the church. What irony that we who have so long burdened you with the guilt of Sodom and Gomorrah find that the fire and brimstone are finally aimed *our* way.

And when Jesus said that foxes have holes and birds have nests but the Son of Man has no place to lay his head, he knew that if ever a day came when churches with their omnipresent crosses of gilded gold thought that now Christ surely had a place to lay his head, he knew that you, my friend, would know better. For with your anguish every night you bear a fearful witness to us all. Until *your* head rests fully welcome within these walls—until then Christ keeps his weary watch *outside* with you, still after all these years aching and envious of foxes and birds.

I hope that you *have* heard, my friend. I tremble for the silent "no" that closes out—and closets in—each day, the quiet daily unmaking of yourself by fears all too well founded. Against all this that you know so well I can offer only words—but maybe this is precisely what I have not done often enough or loud enough or long enough. So, I hope, my unknown friend, that at the end of *this* day, and the next, and on and on, that when you crawl beneath your covers of so much more than linen you remember these words I offer in gentle but firm—unequivocal, strident, flamboyant, audacious—witness: *You are loved by God already now, not "anyway," but fully because of who and how you are.*

And I wait with you for the day when "no" becomes "yes," and you place yourself truthful in our midst. I wait patiently, because who am I to tell you when to step beyond the fears that we have heaped up in your way? And because who am I to think your fear is not, in part indebted to the comfort of my own silence? And I wait *impatiently*, because I know at least this much: that *God is anxious for you to share the joy God takes in the very beauty of who and how you are.*

This essay never appeared in print. I wrote it as an "audition" column for the Notre Dame student newspaper. It earned me a slot as a biweekly columnist the following school year, but because I wrote it the very morning of the fateful Ellen episode, I never had time to distribute before the episode actually aired.

5. The Outing of Ellen: Why All the Fuss?
(April 30, 1997)

Just a few hours from now the seismic culture counters will go haywire as the first lead character in a prime-time TV series comes out of the closet in homes all across America. Needless to say, there's been a bit of a fuss made over this. Some folks plan to boycott the show, the advertisers, even the station; at least one ABC affiliate has declined to air the episode. Many who have welcomed Ellen into their living room quite readily over the past few years will now feel compelled to turn off this woman whose no longer hidden life so turns them off. Others hail this episode as a liberating event, and not just for gays and lesbians. There are plans to celebrate with "Ellen" parties," champagne toasts, and doubtless much more.

I must confess I am not an Ellen devotee. I have seen an episode or two, but I was never captivated by the subtle charm of the show; and, judging from its relatively mediocre ratings, neither have many others.

So, why all the fuss? Is there really something so significant in a somewhat nerdy, somewhat funny, but all in all rather ordinary woman declaring herself lesbian on national TV? I say, yes, precisely because of that last sentence.

Most of us, myself included, have been raised with rather demonized notions of homosexuals. Perverts, queers, effeminate, butch, dyke, intrinsically disordered—and a host of other appellations that would be starred out in this newspaper. They're the sort of folks that send shivers up your spine and make your stomach feel queasy. Like the recent photo in the newspaper of a cow with two faces emerging side by side from the same head. Homosexuals are NOT normal.

Please let us believe that.

If you want to put a lesbian on prime-time TV, at least make her butch, put her on a bike (preferably a Harley), and dress her in leather and chains.

15

But don't suggest that being lesbian (or gay) is so . . . almost boringly normal. I mean, Ellen, aside from whatever she does between the sheets (or in her own imagination) seems just too much like me to write off as "intrinsically disordered" or "unnatural." Her days, her life, are filled with all the same foibles that mark my own. The jams she gets herself into are not all that different from the corners I've painted myself into from time to time. And the simple fact that most viewers have seemed not to notice her (until now) is also a bit like my own experience in the world.

So maybe, just maybe, the fuss over Ellen's coming out is driven less by the fact that she's lesbian than by the concern that she isn't "lesbian" enough to reinforce our own stereotypes of how different and revolting lesbians ought to appear. Maybe there's something in Ellen's ordinariness that calls into question—and at a level hard to defend against—the familiar labels that have always worked to keep homosexuals in their place in our minds.

I may or may not watch Ellen tonight. I imagine I'll jump on the cultural bandwagon—although I'll watch it on tape after bedtime stories with my son are over (not that he wouldn't be allowed to watch it himself, but right now he's far more taken with the adventures of "Maniac Magee" than Ellen). But I don't expect any big surprises myself. Homosexuals became human for me sometime ago. Maybe it was Dale's wry humor; or Dick's ability to imitate Kermit the Frog (or his inability to laugh in any other way than like a Canadian goose); or Kathi's uncommon passion for poetry and literature; or Ken's inability to leave the soap bar somewhere so that the shower spray didn't melt it away. In any case, I've had too many gay and lesbian friends who have been at once so uniquely and ordinarily human that my capacity to consider their sex lives "intrinsically disordered" withered a long time back.

Sure, some folks will respond by saying that I'm confusing apples with oranges, sinners with sins. That you can't argue from the ordinariness of the rest of their lives to justify their sexual desires and actions. Fair enough. But at the very least that ordinariness humanizes them. *It suggests that they deserve neither our demonized fears nor our patronizing pity: they deserve our company, our respect, and our ears to hear from them who they are.* That's a conversation yet to happen on much of this campus and throughout much of this country. If a somewhat

16

nerdy, somewhat funny, lead character on a prime-time TV show nudges us in that direction, well, then I'll tune in for that. The Spirit blows where the Spirit wills; Ellen wouldn't be the first woman of questionable cultural standing to become part of God's divine whimsy. And I don't imagine she'll be the last. Happy viewing!

This piece of poetic commentary dates from my years as a graduate student at the University of Notre Dame—and as a newspaper columnist for The Observer, the Notre Dame student daily. Notre Dame has never known exactly what to do with its gay and lesbian students. It wants to be welcoming without being fully affirming. It has repeatedly refused to offer formal recognition to the student-run support group, GLND/SMC (Gays and Lesbian at Notre Dame/St. Mary's College), and had just recently refused to include sexual orientation in its non-discrimination policy, meaning that the University reserved the right to reject students—or fire faculty and staff—simply because they're gay. Instead, as a sort of "compromise" offer, it had just released an open letter called "The Spirit of Inclusion" in which it uses the words of Ephesians 2:19, "strangers and sojourners no longer," to once again welcome gays and lesbians—but only very conditionally.

The topic had already received a fair bit of press in the student paper, both from other columnists and in campus news stories and letters to the editor. I knew if I wanted to put in my two cents I'd need to find a forum that would be uniquely engaging; thus, the poetry. I should also identify "Monk" as the nickname for Father Ed Malloy, university president at the time. He often signed his name that way, and it was used freely by students and faculty as his name. (I use it because I need a one-syllable word for the meter; it is not at all a mark of disrespect.)

Regarding the poetry itself. Besides offering a style that invites people to keep reading regardless of whether they agree with it, it might be thought of as "guerrilla poetry." The images run so much deeper than the words themselves. They are full of echoes from the gospels and seek to set this issue and these people within the ministry of Jesus. As such the poem steps outside the relative impotence of back and forth reasoned debate. The words ask to become something of Good News themselves, and to the extent this is granted, the poetry itself becomes revelatory.

6. Embracing the Spirit: A Commentary in Rhyme
(September 16, 1997)

It crosses my mind, now and again,
as I take up my proverbial pen,
to author a column composed all in verse,
in metered rhyme my thoughts to rehearse.
You're tired of pointed prose no doubt,
regarding the "Spirit" statement just out.
Well, rest assured, friends, there's no prose this time;
just impassioned thoughts, set all in rhyme.

I write as a male; white, married, and straight—
and friend to a few of less fortunate fate.
I've heard of their anguish and anger quite starkly,

still I speak having seen but "through a glass darkly."
Yet in paradise, when I "see face to face,"
the terror my silence has oft left in place,
though heaven be such that none will need sleep,
tis many of us will be due a good weep.

The issue's complex, but this much is clear,
there's still plenty to fear at the Dome if you're queer.
"'Strangers and sojourners,'" saith the Dome,
"'no longer are you,' please feel right at home.
You'll not be harassed for just being gay;
just mind that your love is not yours to display.
Now if you were married, your love we could praise,
but marriage is sadly off limits to gays.
Still, your kind is fine, and most welcome here . . .
What's that? You want to *act* on your love—oh dear.
Well, the table is set, come join us for dinner.
Each place bears a name—yours is marked 'sinner'."

And yet there is grace in these words of inclusion.
Let your mind run along in creative profusion.
Imagine a National Coming Out Day
held under *this* banner—what could Monk say?
He couldn't protest that it doesn't belong here,
after all, you're now "strangers and sojourners no longer."

And picture in dorm windows, offices, too,
bright colored signs, displayed in full view:
"We've got the Spirit!"—a way to proclaim
a truly safe place here at Notre Dame;
a chorus of signs, in voices united,
"The banquet's much bigger than those so far invited."
Now suppose that these signs for a profit were sold,
by a campus group spirited, inclusive, and bold;
and the money thus raised might be wisely spent
on some inclusive-furthering campus event.

For those whom this spirit moves down to the core,
if you'd like to do just a little bit more,
then take out your wallet or write out a check
to that 501c group known as GLND/SMC ("glend-smeck").
They've nary a nest or a den or a bed;
no place on campus to lay down their head.
I'm sure they'd be grateful your money to juggle
as they faithfully carry on in their struggle.
That address now, for those who are game,
is PO Box 194, Notre Dame.

And lastly an image—and invitation
to queers in our midst to take up your station.
Come tell your stories of wounds all too real;
in the telling itself perhaps many will heal.
As we stand with our doubts, please beckon us near,
to the place where *your* side was pierced by the spear.
And hold up to us your hands and your feet,
bearing the scars where nails and flesh meet.
Like Thomas, we doubt, but be patient and clear;
as we see you before us, perhaps finally we'll hear.
For you, too, are Christ's body; you, too, are Christ's bride.
You, too, have a share in the death that he died.
And you, too, in your loving, amid so much strife,
you carry as well, God's gift of new life.

In the fall of 1998, shortly after arriving at Luther College as a religion instructor and in response to an episode of some anti-gay chalkings during the campus celebration of Coming Out Week, I was asked to speak at a campus forum on Christian perspectives on sexual orientation. This is a slightly expanded version of that talk, which actually began the previous spring (1997) as a talk given at Notre Dame teach-in on homosexuality and the church.

7. Homosexuality and the Newness of God
(November 1998)

When we look to the Bible for guidance about homosexuality, few texts so clutter Christian conversation as the judgment of Sodom and Gomorrah in Genesis 19. So let me begin with a few words about this passage.

I question whether the condemnation of homosexual rape, which is certainly here in this text, can be read as a condemnation of all homosexual activity. Indeed, I question whether homosexual *rape* is even properly an instance of homosexual *activity* anymore than heterosexual rape can be legitimately labeled as heterosexual activity. Rape has more to do with violence and abusive power than with sexuality.

More importantly, I question whether this story is even primarily about the threatened rape. After all, God doesn't destroy them in response to what happens in this text. The angels have come to tell Lot to flee because the divine decree of destruction had already been passed; and it is only incidentally related to the townsmen pounding on the door.

Further, when we look to the rest of the Bible, these cities are only rarely mentioned as guilty of sexual sin. Much more frequently they serve as symbols of gross inhospitality, even of malicious indifference to the vulnerable, of which the homosexual rape of strangers is just one climactic instance.

Isaiah twice likens Israel to Sodom and Gomorrah. In the first instance (1:10-17), the point of comparison becomes clear as he explains what Israel must do to be *no longer* like those cities. He says, "Make justice your aim: redress the wronged, hear the orphan's plea, defend the widow." In the second case (3:9-15), it is God who reveals how Israel is like Sodom saying, "It is you who have devoured the vineyard, the spoils of the poor is in your houses. What do you mean by crushing my people, by grinding the face of the poor?" Ezekiel

(16:49) calls Israel Sodom's "sister," and explains this familial metaphor by noting that Israel, like Sodom, has "plenty of food, and abundant prosperity, but gives no help to the poor and needy." *When the prophets link Israel to Sodom it is because of injustice and indifference to those most vulnerable in the society, not because of preferred sexual partners.*

Jesus shares this view. In Matthew (11:24) he says that even Sodom will have it easier on the day of judgment than those cities which refused to listen to him. But Matthew also explains (11:19) *why* these towns spurned Jesus' message: because he was "a friend of tax collectors and sinners." The point, for Jesus, is not just that Sodom was condemned by God, but that it was condemned for its treatment of the marginal—and yet even it will fare better than those towns who are put off by Jesus' acceptance of those at the social margins.

In a similar passage in Luke (10:12), Jesus again links Sodom to inhospitality. He sends his disciples out preaching, without money or purse or sandals, entrusted entirely to the hospitality of the towns to which they go. When he says that those towns failing to welcome them will fare worse than Sodom on Judgment Day, the parallel is not sexual impropriety. It lies in the horrendous breech of hospitality, the inexcusable indifference toward the vulnerable.

Whether Jesus was aware of Sodom as a town infamous for sexual perversity we do not know. What we do know is that he spoke of it as a city which epitomized the very things his ministry sought to overcome: attitudes and actions which exclude anyone from the community to which God beckons them. It thus becomes a troubling irony that while "sodomy" has come to name the "sin" which the church denounces, it is possible that *in reality "sodomy" is the very inhospitality that the church practices towards homosexuals.*

Indeed, many of the passages in the Bible that have traditionally been used to condemn homosexuality are simply not relevant to the issue as it comes to us today. They condemn something other than consenting same sex persons who desire to build a faithful life together. The Bible simply never addresses *this* concern; it was an unimaginable notion in a time when homosexual *orientation* was unrecognized—and every occasion of homosexual behavior was assumed to be the perverse doing of a heterosexual person. Some of the texts are part of the Old Testament holiness code—a code designed to keep the Israelites separate from other nations—and a code that we today freely ignore except where it happens to support our own prejudices. Such texts are from the story of a people in the midst of coming to be; they are part of a process of revelation, not a final word. Other passages may condemn homosexual rape or the custom of adult men establishing sexual relationships with young boys—a practice common at times in the Greco-Roman world.

Undeniably the biblical writers would be stymied by homosexuality as it confronts the church today. It would strike them, as it strikes us, as something a little too different for most of us to feel comfortable with. But, in my mind, the discomfort that we feel with things so different reflects a fear that entered creation with the Fall. It does *not* reflect the experience of God's unconditional love that empowered Jesus and that seeks to empower us to encounter those different from us in trust, as friends.

In short, the texts used to condemn homosexuality are *contested* passages. There simply is no clear scholarly consensus on how to understand them.

***

The Bible, in the past and still today, has been pressed into the service of racial and ethnic hatred. It has been called on to support slavery and even genocide. It is used to further the suppression of women. It is mined to fuel apocalyptic speculation. Just because it *can* be employed to these ends is no argument that it is legitimately so employed. That a passage has been read one way for centuries *may* say more about the persistent prejudices of the readers—or the writers—of the Bible than about the mind of God.

Some may find it disconcerting that God would allow the Bible to be colored by human biases. But, in fact, any close reading of the Bible will reveal a God who pursues our salvation in the midst of all manner of limitations and even outright difficulties that we, with our assortment of cultural baggage and prejudice, present. The tales of the patriarchs, the Exodus, Israel as a nation, even the early church, are hardly tales of God feeling the need to mediate divine revelation unencumbered by human limitation.

The Incarnation reveals God's willingness to enter history, with all its constraints, in order to encounter us and redeem us. Beyond all the metaphysical musings, it means quite concretely that when Jesus walked the earth he wore sandals and got callused feet. It means that when God's word took on human flesh, that Word willingly bore the marks and limitations of the culture and time in which Jesus lived. And that this did not ultimately limit his ability to reveal God's love and forgiveness. If this is true of Jesus, why should we be surprised that God's written Word might also bear the marks and limitations of the culture and time in which it was written, or is read, without necessarily inhibiting its revelation of God?

To read the Bible as the timeless, pure, unstained word of God is to make it a book by some author other than the God described within it. By saying that I don't mean to simply dismiss the Bible. It portrays a God who never outright dismisses us because of our foibles, but who persistently remains in solidarity with us, patiently—even to the point of the cross—patiently bearing witness to the love which created us and which seeks to redeem us. If we live *with* the Bible, acknowledging its limitations, we can still discover in its pages the God who stands behind them. And I think that is the purpose of the Bible, anyway: not to provide a once-for-all set of moral guidelines, but to offer an introduction to the living God who meets us in the ambiguities of our own lives as well.

***

So who *is* the God we encounter in the Bible? Isaiah provides one succinct answer (43:19). Speaking on behalf of God, Isaiah proclaims to the people in exile, for whom history seems at an end, "Behold, I am doing a new thing." Although the words are spoken some 1500 years into Israel's history and appear well past the halfway mark in the Hebrew Scriptures, they might easily serve as a refrain for every book in the Bible, for every chapter in the history of Israel—and in the history of the church.

One of the fundamental truths that the Bible offers to the question of homosexuality is that the God we encounter is, in the words of Isaiah, "doing a new thing." And not just this once. God is *always* doing a new thing. And we are always forgetting that. The biblical story, in its broadest perspective, tells how God acts for liberation, again and again, in ways utterly beyond the imagination of the Egyptians, the Assyrians, the Babylonians, the Greeks, the Romans (to name just a few of the empires that have been surprised by this God). But it is also—and, for us, more importantly, the story of how God must time and again surprise God's own people, both Jews and Christians, bursting asunder the orthodox boxes that we fashion for this restless deity, this Holy Wind that one moment might unfurl our doctrinal flags in all their pretended brilliance—and then the next moment, in a fit of divine whimsy, might wrap them in a tangled mess around our own ecclesial flagpoles.

Think of Abraham and Sarah, whose child is named Isaac, to recall the disbelieving laughter with which they greeted God's promise of newness. Or Joseph, sold into slavery by his bickering brothers, and then turned into the very means of their blessing and survival.

Think of Israel's constant doubting throughout the Exodus narrative and across the wilderness wanderings; at every turn in the plot they think in despair that they have surely exhausted God's streak of good luck. And at every turn they almost begrudgingly find that God has a new card up the divine sleeve as waters part, manna appears, quails descend, rocks give drink, and walls come tumbling down.

Think of fantastic tale of Jonah—which is fantastic not as a fish story, but as the announcement that God's love extends to nations beyond Israel herself. Think of Isaiah's pronouncement (56:3-8) that foreigners and eunuchs, two classes expressly excluded from the Assembly of Israel by the same holiness code so often used to exclude gays, are now explicitly welcomed as full members of the community of God, as part of what Isaiah names as God's agenda to "gather the outcasts of Israel, and to gather yet others besides those already gathered." Who would have guessed?

On the downside, think of Solomon and the closing of Israel's universe. Israel builds a temple, over the objections of their free-spirited God, claiming to honor God, after the fashion of other nations. But the result—as the prophets repeatedly declare—is that Israel thinks it has domesticated God for its own purposes. From this perspective, what is Exile but a remedial class in theology for a people slow to recognize the perennial newness of God? For it is here that the prophets offer their eschatological visions which spell out "NEWNESS" in all capital letters.

In the Gospels it continues. Jesus welcomes all manner of outcasts from among the Jewish people, feasting with folks the Jews had been raised to despise. After 2000 years we're used to seeing Jesus with such persons—tax collectors, women, sinners—and it doesn't threaten us anymore. But *how dare* he associate with the sort of folks *we've* been raised to despise! And in the early church, think of the Gentiles being welcomed—with no strings attached—into the Jewish Christian community, the early church feeling itself led by the Spirit to widen the circle *even beyond Jesus' own activity*, though not without plenty of protest and turmoil in its own day.

From the first to the last, Israel's encounter with God—and ours—is a tale of unexpected newness, unimagined surprise. God is always about the business of doing a new thing. And surely this has some bearing on whether there is anything new to be said within the church regarding homosexuality.

Finally I see Moses standing in front of the burning bush. He wants a name. "Who shall I say has sent me?" He isn't looking to manipulate God; he isn't trying to gain an advantage of some sort. He just wants to know who he's dealing with; he wants a foothold on which to establish a relationship. "Yahweh," God answers, giving almost an anti-name. It means literally "I am who I am" or "I will be who I will be." In other words, God sets the terms of the relationship as these: "I will burst every box you seek to contain me in. I will defy every limiting definition you devise for me. I will imagine possibilities for you—for us together—which are beyond your wildest dreams. Whatever *you* choose to think of me, *I* will be who I will be. *I am freedom.*"

If the Bible has anything concrete to say about homosexuality it comes by way of what it says about God: that God remains free to surprise us even today. That we dare not imagine that we have yet seen the extent of God's love or the end of God's newness. That to forget this is to be on the verge of idolatry—to fashion an image of a god with nothing new in store for us, a god that merely confirms the half-truths and prejudices with which we're already familiar. That it is therefore a very dangerous thing to declare the compassionate and loving sexual activity of gays and lesbians to be outside the embrace of God.

So, in light of God's perennial newness, how do we encounter one another? In community. In conversation. In vulnerability. What remains consistent across God's ever new involvement with us is the effort to shape us not into individual persons but into a people. From planting the first garden, to pummeling the nation with prophets, to rolling back the stone on Easter morning, God's newness is driven by the desire to bring us into community and conversation.

Our encounters might explore together what it means to live in response to God's gracious love. This becomes *possible* because each of us is redeemed. This remains *necessary* because we remain, each of us, distorted by sin. Each of us, in our sexuality as in other aspects of our lives, is prone to attitudes and actions that fall short of real intimacy with one another. No single orientation or gender has a monopoly on the use of sex to secure physical or emotional benefits for oneself to the detriment of the other person. So we need to speak about ethics and sexuality, *not* lest we be condemned, but precisely *because* we have been redeemed—and redeemed for life in community. We need to talk about fidelity and promiscuity, about mutuality and commitment, about sacramentality and union, and about the profound links between personal sexuality and social justice. We need to reflect about the way our experiences of sexuality inform our experiences of God, redemption, and Christian life.

And these conversations belong not in little enclaves marked off according to our orientations, but as a conversation across our differences, among members of a community united in Christ. I don't say that answers to these questions will come easily. Nor do I presume they will necessarily be the same for all of us, either within or across orientations.

But it is essential that we converse about them *as a community*. This means we must be creative and imaginative—and most of all convivial. We will need to find ways to speak and to listen across chasms of prejudice and fear. We are gathered tonight not on account of trivial matters. For those of you whose lives are marked personally by them, they are matters of dignity and self-worth. I do not downplay that. But if we lose our capacity to be open to the very real fears and concerns of one another, we risk losing also the capacity to invite others to hear us in return. Our strength as Christians ultimately lies not in persuasive rhetoric and airtight argument, but in sharing who we are, from our deepest commitments to our simplest joys, and in manifesting Christ who keeps company with us in these ventures. Indeed, perhaps the best lived-out response to God's gracious love lies less in the answers we discern than in the conversation itself. Because we are called into community by a God who is always doing a new thing, our conversations with one another will never be finished. Life, in the company of an ever-new God flourishes not according to the rigidity of our rules but the conviviality of our conversation.

And, we should expect to be surprised by how it all plays out. Pharaoh *was* humiliated despite his many chariots. Yet Cyrus willingly, if unwittingly, became God's instrument of restoration. And the king of Nineveh publicly repented and called on his administration and all his subjects to do the same. Thus, I think we should approach the future with confidence . . . and with a grand sense of irony. What seems like a momentous occasion may be a small step in a very long walk. What seems like an insignificant event might prove decisive. And what seems like a devastating defeat may turn out to be the prelude to victory.

***

Finally, I will close with a word from my own spiritual experience. When Peter and John were reprimanded by the Jewish authorities for preaching the gospel in Jerusalem, they replied, "We cannot but speak of what we have seen and heard." So it is with me, finally. I have seen gays and lesbians in relationships every bit as blessed with joy and love as those of any heterosexual couples I know. I have heard the almost unfathomable anguish of gays and lesbians as they try to find dignity in the midst of a Church determined to deny it to them. And, perhaps most importantly, *I have heard the gospel from gays and lesbians.* I have heard them, at various moments in my life, speaking genuine, God-inspired Good News to me or to others. I have seen them, in essence, casting out demons in Jesus' name, even though they stand outside the accepted community of Christ. When the disciples complained to Jesus

28

about this very thing, he said simply, "Whoever is not against me, is with me."

If God is not embarrassed or ashamed to work and speak through their sexually-active-gay-and-lesbian-lives, then it is I who must be embarrassed or ashamed for a church which is neither willing nor able to see this. When Jesus spoke of persons who have ears but cannot hear and eyes but cannot see, I can think of no contemporary issue that more clearly reflects this. *Already* sitting alongside us in the pews on every Sunday morning are gay people, just as anxious and joyful as we are to hear the Gospel—although, thanks to us, they may be uncertain as to how much it applies to them. *Already* alongside us at the communion rail lesbians hold out their cupped hands to receive the same body of Christ that we receive, the same forgiveness, the same promise of new life—although thanks to us, they may be uncertain as to whether the meal bears God's promise to them. And *already*, preaching to us or presiding over the sacrament, however well-hidden in the closet and behind the clerical collar, untold numbers of homosexuals serve God by ministering to us, preaching Good News and celebrating the Eucharist. We would prefer not to see and not to hear—but we should be at least this clear: *it is the very power of the Spirit of God upon which we turn our backs.*

I need to say this not just for my sake, though it is important to my own integrity. I need to say it for Ken and Brian, for Paul and Dannie, and for Dale and Ruth and Dick and Kathi and Bonnie—who are just some of the gay and lesbian persons that I have numbered among my friends. I would be less than a friend to be silent. And I need to say it because my own experience of Spirit-driven discipleship compels me to continue banqueting with those persons that the world or the church still prefers to name as outcasts. And I can tell you this, speaking from personal experience, *when you feast with gays and lesbians you will find that you are feasting with Jesus as well.*

29

This essay was first presented as a lecture to my students in "Introduction to Bible" at Luther College. I've left it in exactly that format; you can imagine Debbie's surprise. Here, for the first time, I begin to move decisively beyond simply treating the biblical passages most frequently used to address the morality of homosexuality.

8. The Bible and Homosexuality
(May 4, 2000)

The specific topic for today is "The Bible and Homosexuality." More generally speaking, the issue is how we appropriately move from biblical texts to ethical perspectives. And ultimately my presentation will offer some thoughts on how the Bible enlightens our perspective not just on homosexuality but on sexuality in general. I won't pretend that my presentation today is neutral. I'm not at all certain that "neutral" scholarship is really possible, but on this topic in particular the stark reality is that every time it is discussed, lives hang in the balance. That doesn't excuse sloppy scholarship; it does mean that however well-grounded my scholarship is, it is also undeniably passionate. And I won't apologize for that.

Lastly, let me be clear from the start about the context out of which I approach this topic. I'm straight. I have had a long history of close friendships with gay and lesbian persons so I hardly come to this topic without my own biases.

We begin on my Listserv. Debbie, you've known since late February that this day was coming, so while you slink down into your seat, at least perk your ears up. It's time to take up your question about a ruthless God.

Midway through February, one of my students, Debbie, posted a comment on my Listserv, noting that the God described in many Old Testament passages seems, well, rather ruthless. And ever quick to endear herself to me, Debbie also observed that in my treatment of such passages I seemed to be—and I quote here—"manipulating the God of the Old Testament to be the God we want to believe in, not the God that He is." Let me be clear on two things at this point: first, Debbie did not make these remarks as a vindictive accusation, she raised the issue with genuine sincerity; second, I don't repeat them here either to embarrass Debbie or to deftly dismiss her concern. I repeat her words because she has succinctly and bluntly set forth the terms under which today's conversation must proceed.

Is God ruthless? And if we say No, *are* we simply imagining a God more to our liking?

Picture this. You're gay—or lesbian. You sit in church on a Sunday morning. Worse yet, you've volunteered to read the lessons for the day. You approach the lectern and find yourself reading these words from Leviticus (20:13): "If a man lies with a male as with a woman, both of them have committed an abomination; they shall be put to death." Or perhaps the text is I Corinthians 6:9-10: "Do you not know that wrongdoers will not inherit the kingdom of God? Do not be deceived! Fornicators, idolaters, adulterers, male prostitutes, sodomites. . .—none of these will inherit the kingdom of God." Or maybe the words come from Romans 1: "God gave them up to degrading passions. Their women exchanged natural intercourse for unnatural and in the same way also the men, giving up natural intercourse with women, were consumed with passion for one another." When you're done reading, the church bulletin instructs you to conclude with the phrase: "This is the word of the Lord." And what do you do now? Remember, you're gay or lesbian. Do you go on to say, Well, brothers and sisters in Christ, meet me outside after the service—and brings rocks? Do you quietly excuse yourself from church—and never return?

I take it as a given that today we recognize that biologically, psychologically, and—in our better moments—spiritually, our sexuality (whether straight or otherwise) is absolutely intrinsic to our person. It is surely *not* the singular defining quality of our selfhood, but it is hardly an optional feature. It *does* sit at the heart of who we are. Then for gays and lesbians these passages *do* speak of a ruthless God. And any effort to pretend otherwise is an insidious deception.

So there *is* a short answer to the first question regarding the Bible's stance on homosexuality. The Bible does *not* offer any words of explicit affirmation of same-gender sexual relationships. And wherever it does mention same-gender sexual relationships it does so with a less than friendly tone. Now let

31

me be very clear: I *don't* think this is the last word we can speak on this, but it is the *first* word, and we need to be honest about that.

We *do* have these texts. What do we do with them?

I think the real issue here is not to ask what these passages actually say about homosexuality but to ask first and foremost how do we understand Scripture? If you have read the pieces by Dan Spencer and myself in your course packets, you will see that at the very least these are all "contested passages," that is, they are verses over which there is plenty of dispute as to their exact meaning. But more and more I am less and less sure that it is sufficient to play that card, so to speak. Because to focus on the issue of whether we've properly understood them yet, whether we have them set in their proper historical context, whether we have figured out with reasonable clarity what the actual words originally meant, all of this still implicitly assumes that these words are divinely-inspired and that once we get clear on what they meant to their original authors we'll have figured out God's view as well. Then maybe God isn't telling us to stone homosexuals per se, maybe the issue in Leviticus, for instance, is really temple prostitution. In other words, maybe not every faggot has to die, just those connected to pagan temples. But the text does pretty unmistakably imply that it's time to collect rocks. And I get queasy with the notion of a God who orders anyone's death, let alone the death of a whole category of people.

Me? What do I do as I sit in that imaginary church scene described above? I sit in the pew and weep, because it seems to me that we have canonized a book that in some places simply fails to capture the truth of God. Indeed, it seems to me that it is a text which in some places bears sad witness to the willingness of *ruthless people* to hoist their prejudices all the way up to heaven and transcribe them into the heart of God.

I suggest this not out of disrespect for the Bible, but out of profound *respect* for this book, a respect that is so profound that it sometimes forces me to deal with more ambiguity than I might care to. And out of a profound respect for God that refuses to let me assume that any written text can fully contain the character of God, that any letters penned by the human hand and crafted by the human mind can set boundaries for the One who responded to Moses' query by saying, "I will be who I will be."

So, to one part of your question, I would say, Yes, Debbie, we are stuck—just as were the original biblical authors—with the task of imagining God as best we can, while remembering that neither we—nor they—are going to get it exactly right. This suggests that any move from biblical texts to ethical perspectives must be much more nuanced than simply readings our morals off the printed page.

We heard in the video two weeks ago about the dispute between John's circle of believers and the Jews who did not accept Jesus as Messiah. John frames this dispute rhetorically as a conflict over the Word of God. Most Jews had identified the Word of God as the written Torah, but John's assertion was that the Word of God is a living presence, embodied historically in Jesus of Nazareth and now present to the church through its sacraments. Ironically, Christians today are often most comfortable with the notion of a written Word, an unchanging text. But John's view of a living dynamic Word is hardly unique in the early church. Mark (2:22) has Jesus say that "No one puts new wine into old wine skins" lest the wine burst the skins. And Matthew (25:40) records Jesus' telling his disciples that they will find him now not in a written text but "in the least of those" around them, in clothing the naked, feeding the hungry, and so forth. Is it then too much to suggest that Jesus might say today that as often as we hear the anguish of our gay and lesbian brothers and sisters we hear the anguish of Jesus himself?

Jeremiah charged the members of the Israelite establishment with a miscalculation of the worst sort when they presumed that somehow on account of the Temple they had God at their beck and call. He mocked the false security they claimed in chanting like a mantra, "This is the Temple of the Lord . . . This is the Temple of the Lord." Today it is tempting for us to pick up a similar chant and repeat together, "This is the Word of the Lord . . . This is the Word of the Lord." But Jeremiah's intuition—and mine as well—is that there *is* a certain genuine ruthlessness to God's character, but that it is expressed in *ruthless freedom* and in *ruthless love*. And that it is ruthless precisely in challenging the prejudices by which we prefer to set boundaries for it. And

33

that it is especially ruthless in challenging the presumptions of the powerful because their prejudices have the greatest capacity to inflict suffering.

One of Jesus' parables (Mt. 18:23-35) tells of a person in debt way over his head. He's about to be thrown into prison, but at the last minute, in an act of pure grace, the creditor forgives the debt in its entirety and the man is off the hook. The first thing he does is encounter another person who owes him money and rather than mirror the unexpected forgiveness he has just received, he threatens to jail this other debtor. The point is that the God who forgives us so much will be less than pleased if we fail to echo that forgiveness to others.

Let me ask a question: Do we have any Jews in the room? I didn't think so. Okay, then these words are for all of you here. Listen to what God supposedly instructs Israel to do to those persons living in the land of Canaan as Israel enters it (cf. Josh. 6:21; 8:25-26; 10:28-40, esp. v. 40). And let's be very clear on this, I do mean *persons*. I mean folks who laughed and cried and worked hard and made love and raised families. I mean *real* persons. According to the biblical narrative God says, in so many words, "Kill them. *Kill them all.*" Why? Just because they're not Jews.

Friends, it is only by the luck of the geographical draw that none of our ancestors lived in Canaan. Because if they had, these verses would've dictated a death sentence for each and every one of us. Because not one of us is Jewish. And in these verses, just being born Gentile is cause enough to be killed.

Deuteronomy (23:3), Ezra (9:1), and Nehemiah (13:3) are all less harsh, but each of these texts contains passages that are equally clear. Simply on account of how we are born, we are forbidden to join the Assembly of God, forbidden to be part of the official congregation of God's chosen people. It's not just that we can't be "ordained." We can't even join in worship. We can't even raise our families in the same neighborhood.

Well, Third Isaiah (56:3-8), and Ruth, and Jonah, all challenge this exclusivity. And although the issue crops up again (in a somewhat different form) in the early church, it has so long been settled—*of course* Gentiles are welcomed by God—that we easily forget what an enormous debt (the simple fact of our not being Jews) has been "forgiven" us, and so we are quick to encounter other debtors (say, those who are not straight) and hope to exact from them the full measure called for by Scripture oblivious to the grace shown to us. If we care to read Jesus' parable in all its pointedness (which I, for one, don't care to . . . but if we did) then God is right now stoking the fires of hell not for homosexuals but for those of us who have proven unwilling to mirror for them the grace we Gentiles so willingly receive for ourselves.

Do we have a ruthless God? My answer is No. But the measure of our own sin can be seen in our unwillingness to break free from an understanding of Scripture that upholds an image of a ruthless God—especially that of a God who is ruthless toward those too different from and with less power than ourselves. Too often we do with Scripture what the Israelites were so tempted to do with the Temple: we use it to domesticate God, to tame the fierceness of God's freedom into something we can predict, something we can control, something we can count on to be on "our" side.

On the other hand, I have to say that Yes, in a manner of speaking, we do have a ruthless God. But it is a God of ruthless love and ever widening inclusivity. And a God who is consistently on the side of the victims of history. (Granted, this *can* be read by those victims as a God who is ruthlessly against their oppressors, but I think it is quite possible for God to despise oppression without despising the persons caught up in it on either the top or the bottom.) From the original choice of a wandering nomad as the father of a nation to the collection of barren women, unloved wives, younger children, and slaves, this is a God who time and again chooses to include persons that we must assume don't belong in the story. Later on Gentiles will be welcomed. In Jesus' ministry we have another whole set of outcasts unexpectedly—almost unimaginably—drawn into the circle of God's love.

So, the movement from biblical text to ethical perspective happens best not via specific passages but by discerning overarching themes. And it involves us in the imaginative task of constructing a portrait of the God revealed in these themes. God's Word shapes our ethics by refusing to remain a fixed word on the page, but rather by insisting on becoming a living Presence in our midst, a New Wine quite able to burst old assumptions, a new voice waiting to be heard in the least of those around us.

I do think, Debbie, it *is* fair to ask whether we end up simply imagining a God more to our liking? But I think it is also fair to push this question further. Is it really "easier" or more "convenient" to imagine a God who is relentlessly inclusive? A God who challenges us again and again not to judge our enemies but to love them, not to condemn those who are outcast but to welcome them? Does that image of God really water down who God is, or does it threaten to undercut so entirely the patterns of prejudice with which we insulate our lives that, far from making God more palatable, *it just plain scares the shit out of us.* Because if such a God really expects us to live *imago Dei,* in God's image, echoing God's radical love in the world, well, we see in Jesus how the world treats those who seek to embody such radical love—and it isn't easy or convenient.

Okay, if I can look to the wider biblical witness about God's surprising and inclusive love as a vantage point from which to affirm the integrity of gay and lesbian persons as persons embraced by the love of God, can I say anything about God's expectations for sexual ethics among homosexual or bisexual persons? Yes. I think to do so we need to consider what we can gather about God's expectations for *all* expressions of sexual intimacy.

Here, I think it is helpful to begin with the simple observation that in Hebrew the same verb can mean both "to know" and "to make love to." It is as though the Hebraic mind intuited at least this much, that loving and knowing are overlapping realities. That which we know without loving, we dominate and desecrate. That which we love without knowing, we depersonalize and trivialize. The fullness of knowing culminates in loving—and vice versa. This is what the Hebrew language intimates at the very bodily level. When two persons, enfleshed, gifted with five senses and an irrepressible hunger for intimacy, when two such persons make love to one another, truly they *know* one another with all of their senses—indeed with all of their person: psychic, emotional, and spiritual, as well as physical.

So sexual loving is a profound expression of knowing. And in some sense, sexual ethics is an ethics of knowledge. The question is, How do we *know* well?

I think this is an insightful way to frame the issue because this same wordplay over knowing and making love has echoes in how the prophets describe our relationship with God. Jeremiah at one point (22:15-16) asks the very question, What does it mean to know God? And his question, pointedly put to the King could be provocatively rendered, *What does it mean to make love to Yahweh, to caress God?* What does it look like when we—enfleshed human persons, with five senses, along with our emotional hungers and psychic longings—when we know God with our whole persons, bodies and all? Jeremiah answers his own question. It looks like this: justice—especially for the weakest among us. Amos, Isaiah, Micah all echo this intuition. God is known—and loved—in acts of mercy and justice. When we look at Jesus we see this prophetic insight enacted: Jesus knows God by caring for those around him, especially those in need.

Then, to return to our question of sexual ethics, I think this much is essential: appropriate bodily knowing—expressions of sexual intimacy that will be pleasing to God—must pass the measure of justice and mercy. Sexual intimacy must not be exploitive of power differences, whether based on money, age, race, gender, or social role. For *any* sexual intimacy (straight or otherwise) to be ethical it must *not* transgress justice; it *must* embody mercy as the compassionate nurture of the other.

Beyond this, I think there are a few other guidelines to be set. But only a few. I draw the following from a reflection on the way the Scriptures overall image the relationship of intimacy between God and God's people, taking that as my reference point for a model of human intimacy, grounded in the conviction that we are called to live lives which are *imago Dei*, in the image of God. Interestingly, along these same lines, Luther remarked that *real* marriage is the intimate mystical union that exists between Christ and the believer. *Human* marriages are real or authentic marriages in Luther's view only insofar as they echo the features of marital union with Christ. (Ironically then, although I don't argue that Luther himself would follow his imagery through this way,

37

this suggests that any marriage I enter as a straight man with a woman is *real* only insofar as it echoes the really true marriage I already enjoy as a man with a man, Jesus.) Anyway, on to my short list.

First, *fidelity*, that is, *practiced faithfulness*. Sexual intimacy is among the deepest expressions of self-vulnerability that we can engage in. To do so outside the context of genuine, promised fidelity is neither wise nor safe. It carries us to the precipice of psychic, emotional, and even physical destructiveness. On the other hand, to offer and to receive such vulnerability in the midst of fidelity is truly to stand on holy ground. I do not think this dictates that from our first date we need to pledge strict fidelity. I do think it suggests that as the level of physical intimacy in a relationship rises, it must be met with an equal increase in professed—and practiced—fidelity.

Second, *an openness to a shared life*. Not every dating relationship will develop into a committed relationship that attempts a lifelong expression. Nonetheless, as an embodiment of deeply personal knowing, sexuality is not a sort of fast food pursuit. It unfolds like a multi-course dinner, in stages, over time, with assorted flavors and textures to be savored slowly along the way. Though our sexual expression will have a natural time of self-discovery and exploration, ultimately it is situated as one feature of who we are across the whole of our lives. To pursue sexual intimacy at length, as though it might be compartmentalized from the rest of our being, displays a lack of fidelity to our self.

Third, it seems more than coincidence that sexual intimacy, such deeply mutual knowing, can be biologically *procreative*. By observing this I am *not* suggesting that homosexual relationships—or straight relationships—in which physical reproduction is not a biological option are somehow deficient. I *am* suggesting that the character of healthy mutual erotic knowing will be such that it spills into the wider world in ways that nurture creation. In a real sense, this merely reflects my conviction that the measure of justice in a sexual relation is larger than how the partners regard one another; it is also concerned with how they, together, care for the world around them with whatever gifts they have to offer.

And fourth, and perhaps most often overlooked or skipped over in awkward silence, sexual intimacy is appropriately expressed with *joyful abandon*. In a metaphorical example, when King David welcomes the ark of the covenant into Jerusalem (II Sam. 6:14-16, 20-22) his intimacy with God is such that he dances before the ark with joyful abandon, even to the point that he flashes the crowds with the royal jewels, so to speak. More directly, quite independent of any symbolic reading you give to it, the Song of Songs is a wide-eyed, nothing-held-back celebration of the joyful capacity that our bodied selves have to become gracious gifts one to another.

There is a rabbinic tradition which says that at the Last Judgment we will be required to give an account for only one thing: that is, for whichever of God's good gifts we haven't partaken in gratitude. God will ask each of us, Have you felt the wonder of a rainbow spread out across the sky? How about the quiet breath of a sleeping baby? Have you crackled your way through the autumn leaves? Gazed up in awe at the twinkling stars? And had the patience to wait for—and gasp at—a streaking meteorite? Can you describe for me the taste of fresh blackberries still warm from the sunlight? Now tell me about the sweet taste of a kindness shown to a person in need. Yes, and have you relished the ecstatic pleasure of one enfleshed person knowing another with joyful abandon? The rabbis sensed that if you had not savored such good gifts as these, you'd better have a good excuse. They would agree with Alice Walker, who has one of her characters say, "I think it pisses God off if you walk by the color purple in a field somewhere and don't notice it."

In closing, let me come back to my initial question, can the Bible affirm active loving gay and lesbian relationships? At the level of specific texts, No, because the Bible is bound by historical, cultural, and simply prejudicial human limits even as it seeks to express the truth of God. At the level of overarching themes, Yes, because the Bible declares that God's love ranges wider and further than we have yet seen. And from the perspective of actual ethical guidelines, I think we answer the question by framing it this way: Given that these reflections on the biblical narrative suggest that God desires that our sexual intimacy reflect the features of justice, mercy, and fidelity, an openness to a shared life, the nurture of creation, and joyful abandon, can gay and lesbian relationships be *imago Dei*, can they bear the image God in these ways? I think the answer is a resounding *Yes*.

This essay is adapted from a sermon I preached at Luther College during morning chapel. It would be an understatement to say I was nervous beforehand, but the text assigned for the day (Joel 2:28-29) opened a doorway that I could not help but walk through.

9. Pentecost: The Season of Anything but Ordinary Time
(November 17, 2000)

Pentecost is the longest—and probably least understood season in the liturgical year. We're pretty clear on what the Advent-Christmas-Epiphany cycle is about. And we're fairly certain about how Lent, Holy Week, and Easter fit together. But Pentecost—some tongues of flame, a bunch of languages . . . and then what? Then we slip into the season of Pentecost, sometimes referred to in liturgical circles as "ordinary time."

But for the early church this time was far from ordinary. For them, the experience of Pentecost meant being drawn full force into "extraordinary time." It meant living into the complicated ecstasy of Joel's vision (2:28-29): "Then afterward I will pour out my spirit on all flesh; your sons and your daughters shall prophesy, your old men shall dream dreams, and your young men shall see visions. Even on the male and female slaves, in those days, I will pour out my spirit." Pentecost is a season of anything but "ordinary time"!

Pentecost, not just as a one-Sunday festival but as a long unfolding season should be treasured by those of us committed to opening the church to GLBT persons. *Pentecost is the liturgical season for the church in ferment.* Remember that while Joel's vision sounds wonderful, the actual experience sparked a good bit of contention in the church at Corinth. God's fierce whimsy in pouring out the Spirit—even on slaves for God's sake!—resulted in a wildfire-diversity of spiritual gifts that left the community bickering over whose gifts were best—and whose gifts were best set aside. In chapters 12 and 13 of I Corinthians we see Paul ransack his theological imagination in an effort to respond to this, employing first the powerful metaphor of the human body and its many parts and later composing his eloquent hymn to love. His words aim to help the church of his day keep the gospel at the center of its life in the midst of the "extraordinary" season of Pentecost.

Perhaps nowhere in the church is the ambiguity of Joel's prophesied blessing of the Spirit felt more keenly today than in our efforts to harmonize the diversity of spiritual gifts evident when Holy Breath meets tactile flesh in the mystery of human sexuality. What if we could hear Paul's message with new clarity today? Listen . . .

Chapter 12: (1) Now, concerning the good spiritual gifts of sexuality, brothers and sisters, I do not want you to be uninformed. (2) You know that apart from spiritual reverence, you can easily be led astray into dark emptiness, however deep your momentary pleasure. (3) Therefore I want you to understand that no one, making love within the goodness of God's joy ever says "my partner is merely a means to my pleasure," and no one can say "my partner is to me the very goodness of God" except by the Holy Spirit.

(4) Now there are varieties of sexual gifts but the same Spirit; (5) and there are varieties of loving, but the same Divine Lover; (6) and there are varieties of creating, but it is the same Joyful Creator who inspires them all in every one. (7) To each is given the manifestation of the Spirit for the good of the whole community. (8) To one is given through the Spirit the love of a woman for a woman, and to another the love of a woman for a man by the same Spirit, (9) to another the love of a man for a man, to another the love of man for a woman, (10) to another the love of a man for a man or a woman, to another the love of woman for a woman or a man, to another the riddled wonder of gender perplexity, to another the love of all within the gift of celibacy. (11) All these are inspired to love by one and the same Spirit, who bestows such gifts according to Wisdom and Mystery.

(12) For just as the body is one and has many members, and all the members of the body, though many, are one body, so it is with the community of God's children. For by one Spirit we were all baptized into one body—lesbian and straight, gay and bisexual, transgender and celibate—and all were bathed in the joy and grace of one Spirit.

(14) For the body does not consist of one member but of many. (15) If the gay man should say, "Because I am not straight, I do not belong to the body," that would not make him less a part of the body. (16) And if the bisexual woman should say, "Because I am not lesbian, I do not belong to the body," that would not make her less a part of the body. (17) If the whole body were straight, where would be the beauty of gay love? If the whole body were lesbian, where would be the wonderment of those who are transgender? (18) But as it is, God has arranged the orientations in the body, each one of them, as Divine Wisdom saw fit. (19) If all were of a single orientation, where would the wholeness of the body be?

(20) As it is, there are many ways of being sexual, yet one body of God's people. (21) The celibate person cannot say to the sexually active one, "I have no need of you," nor again can the straight person say to the bisexual "I have no need of you." (22) On the contrary, the parts of the body which seem less important are indeed indispensable, (23) and it is those parts of the body which are most vulnerable that we invest with the greatest care, (24) care which our less vulnerable parts may not require. For God has so composed the body that we should offer the greatest consideration to those members most exposed to peril, (25) that there should be neither discord nor damage within the body, but that the members might mutually care for one another. (26) If one member is marginalized, let all lament together; if one member is fulfilled, let all rejoice.

(27) Now you are altogether the body of God's presence in the world, and each one of you individually is a member of it. (28) And God has appointed within the church that there should be gay and lesbian, straight and celibate, bisexual and transgender. (29) Are all gay? Are all lesbian? Are all straight? Are all celibate? (30) Are all bisexual? Are all transgender? (31) Of course not! But desire earnestly to discern the gift that is yours.

And I will show you a still more excellent way, one which unites all these gifts unto the glory of God.

Chapter 13: (1) If I can woo all those whom I find attractive with the sweetness of my words, but have not love, I am a noisy gong or a clanging cymbal. (2) And if I have physical beauty myself beyond measure, and if I exude confidence so as to draw all persons unto me, but have not love, I am nothing. (3) If I devote myself to the art of physically pleasuring another, but have not love, I offer them nothing and gain nothing for myself.

(4) Love is patient and kind; it cares for the needs and celebrates the joys of the other in good cheer. Love is not jealous or boastful; it seeks neither to possess the other nor to honor exclusively the self. (5) It is not arrogant or rude, irritable or resentful. Love does not insist on its own way, but revels in the intricate mysteries that make the other unique. Love takes its deepest joy in knowing the other as an irreplaceable and unmistakable child of God. (6) It does not rejoice at wrong, even when wrong benefits the self. It rejoices in the right, in the consummation of mutual care between any of God's creatures. (7) Love bears all things—with transforming perseverance. Love believes all things—with prophetic passion. Love hopes all things—confident in God's good care. Love endures all things—firm in solidarity when change does not come soon.

(8) Love never ends; as for physical beauty, it will fade with years yet to live; as for wit, it will dim with age; as for confidence, it will falter with infirmity. (9) For our beauty and our wit and our confidence are all incomplete in this life; (10) but when God's final Wisdom holds sway such incompleteness will give way to that which is Complete. (11) When I was a youth I spoke and thought and reasoned like a youth—and it was well with me. But when I grew up I saw all things quite differently, and I perceived how incomplete were my youthful ways. (12) For now, our sexual joy, however rich, is still only a dim reflection of what it shall be like when we see our beloved face to face. Now we know those to whom we pledge our deepest fidelity—even in our best moments we know them only in part; then, by the astonishing grace of God, we shall know them fully, even as we find ourselves fully and graciously known.

(13) So the varieties of sexual gifts run as wide as the Spirit's whimsy, but uniting each particular gift with its beloved, and with the community, and with God, is this singular gift: love.

To which I can only add, Amen!

43

This short piece ran as a letter to the editor at Luther College. It was a response to a letter the previous week from a pastor who was promoting "reparative therapy," a type of behavior modification that claims to "cure" homosexuality. I haven't included his letter here, but I think you can follow mine without having read his.

10. Who Needs Curing? A Response to Reparative Therapy
(April 13, 2002)

Last week Rev. Rodel Eberle defended Christian attempts to "cure" homosexual persons. As an instructor of religion, deeply committed to keeping the company of Jesus, and privileged to count many gay, lesbian, and bisexual persons as my friends, I want to respond.

Virtually everything Eberle says of homosexuality is, in fact, true of hetero*sexism (which is not* identical with hetero*sexuality*). *Consider:* heterosexism is the dominant assertion of heterosexuality as the *only* acceptable sexual expression. Whether grounded in ignorance, fear, or malice, *heterosexism is sin.* It is responsible for broken relationships, for suicides, and for violence against GLBT persons. Heterosexism, in the words of Romans 1:25, "exchanges the truth of God for a lie, and worships the creature rather than the Creator." Anxious over anatomy instead of honoring the sexual diversity that reflects the rampant glory of God, heterosexism is neither easy nor comfortable to overcome, but with the power of the gospel it is possible. The goal of overcoming it is not to make straight persons gay; it is to free them from the compulsion, conscious or otherwise, to violate the dignity of others, a compulsion often driven by their own sexual and spiritual insecurity.

Eberle recalls the saying that "no one in their right mind would choose to be homosexual," arguing that therefore therapeutic help should be offered to ease their suffering. No. It is the persistent assault on the integrity of homosexuals by both church and society that bears the largest responsibility for their psychological suffering. Indeed this is precisely the position of the American Psychiatric Association, the American Psychological Association, the American Medical Association, and the American Academy of Pediatrics (you can find each of their respective statements on the web). Thus, it is church and society that should be called to account. Homosexuals do not need to be cured. *Heterosexuals intent on making heterosexuality a monopoly need "curing."* They cause the harm. They inflict the wounds. Jesus' harshest rebukes are aimed at those who lay impossible burdens on the souls of others.

Eberle alludes to Luther's "liberal" atmosphere as part of the problem and writes, "probably you have guessed that I am a conservative." Well, if you have read the gospels carefully, then to paraphrase Eberle, probably you have guessed that, far from being a conservative (or a liberal) I am a friend of Jesus. And I hear in Jesus a message that *does* bring with it the power to overcome anything that makes us miserable. But it is not a message that calls homosexuals to reject the unique expression of love granted them by God. It is a message that empowers them to resist—and to overcome—the forces of heterosexist prejudice. It is a message that invites them to rejoice in the unconditional love of God and to dare to love one another with confidence and with integrity. It is a message in which we might all "live and move and have our being"—but never at the expense of others.

The "hallmark" of Christianity, both individually and corporately, is *not*, as Eberle suggests, strict "adherence to the voice of Scripture." It is adherence to the freedom of God, to the voice of Love. Scripture is worth quoting when and where it vividly bears witness to this deep mystery of Surprising Love. At one such place it says, "Behold I am doing a new thing (Is. 43:19). I am gathering in to my people others who have not yet been gathered in (Is. 56:8)." The "hallmark" of Christianity is *Good News.* And if you're gay, lesbian, bisexual, or transgender, it is Good News *for you.* Without any strings attached. So, if you're Christian, welcome home.

This text, never developed beyond outline form, is from a presentation I made for an Augsburg College Panel on Christianity and Homosexuality. Although many of the ideas here appear elsewhere in these essays, this offers a very nice, concise overview of my thoughts.

11. Where I'm at as a Christian & Why I'm There
(October 9, 2002)

Where I'm at as a Christian: For better or for worse—and I'm inclined to think that ultimately it's for the better—this is an issue in which we are beholden more to our hearts than to our minds. Changes in perspective here seldom, if ever, occur at the level of logical argument. So my remarks today—and the reasons I offer—are intended less to be logically persuasive to you than to be faithfully representative of my heart.

(1) Sexual Orientation is a mystery. Stemming from an intricate interplay of nature and nurture, genetics and environment, sexual orientation seems to become relatively set at a very early age, long before our adolescent hormones kick in. No legitimate research indicates that sexual orientation is a conscious choice that any of us can make—or unmake—by effort or therapy.

(2) The Bible's place in this debate is largely misplaced. The passages most often quoted to condemn homosexuality in fact offer no direct guidance regarding consensual same-sex Christian relationships. There are simply no biblical passages which can be read to unambiguously condemn these types of relationships. The Bible has a profound contribution to make in the realm of sexual ethics in general and at the point of embracing sexuality as a good gift. But we, as a church, are largely disinterested in listening to it on these scores.

(3) Gay, lesbian, bisexual, and transgender persons, regardless of how uncomfortable I may (or may not) feel with their bedroom behavior, their public affections, or their private fantasies, are every bit as loved and accepted by God as I am—amid all the endearing qualities and questionable aspects of *my* bedroom behavior, *my* public affections, and *my* private fantasies.

(4) Therefore, I am convinced that the church ought to welcome them, listen to them, learn from them, ordain them, bless their unions, embrace

their sorrows, and in general offer them holy companionship through the whole of their lives.

Why I'm there.

(1) I am not an expert by any means on the science of sexuality, but from the reading I've done, it seems pretty clear that our sexuality—whether heterosexual, homosexual, bisexual, or transgender—is far from being clearly understood. If we claim to speak from a scientific vantage point and in a tone other than humility, we slip almost immediately into arrogance.

(2) I am not a biblical scholar, but my biblical training in college, seminary, and graduate school has given me a pretty fair ability to follow the scholarly debates on the texts in question. I don't think either side can make a 100% conclusive claim as to how the handful of passages in question should be read. It seems obvious to me that these passages are so far from clear that our interpretations of them are inevitably colored by prejudice. I choose to be colored by the prejudice of God's love rather than by what strikes me as the prejudice of human fear.

(3) Further, if the Bible is not clear on the issue of homosexuality, it is very clear on the claim that God's love for persons persistently outstrips our imagination. Jonah can't imagine that God loves Ninevites, but the book of Jonah declares otherwise. Ezra and Nehemiah can't imagine God loves Moabites, but the book of Ruth declares otherwise. Leviticus can't imagine God welcomes eunuchs, but Isaiah declares otherwise. Jesus' contemporaries can't imagine that God loves Samaritans, but Jesus declares otherwise. Peter can't imagine that God accepts uncircumcised Gentiles as Christians—until first Paul and then a divine vision convince him otherwise. If there is one theme that ought to be eminently clear from the biblical story it is that God reserves the right to include more people in the kingdom than we thought we saw on the invitation list.

(4) Besides these examples, Christians have particular reasons to stand in a relationship of peculiar freedom regarding written texts.

In Matthew 18 (vv. 18-19) Jesus gives his followers authority to "bind and loose." This term appears in rabbinic Judaism as the authority rabbis have to decide about any matters not previously discussed in detail—or to reconsider the decisions made by those before them. We are heirs to a *living* tradition. This is, in fact, what Paul's letters consistently do, often in pretty radical ways. We ought to be following his example rather than simply quoting his early efforts. However the church exercises its authority to "bind and loose," it cannot do so in the Spirit of Christ until it frees itself of the limitations (not the guidance) of the written texts and listens well to the presence of Christ in the least of these, our GLBT brothers and sisters. Only then—and not before—can we bind and loose in love.

In John's gospel (1:14) we hear that "the Word became flesh," but we often forget that John is writing against the backdrop of Jewish neighbors who have rejected Jesus and have instead pledged their total fidelity to the written Torah. John rallies his Jewish Christian readers by declaring that in Jesus they know a Word that jumped off the written page, stepped into our midst, burst asunder the many boxes that had been built to contain God, and refused to go away, even when a stone was rolled in front of the tomb. Today we still believe that beyond any written text we are gifted with the living presence of Christ in our midst.

At the end of Matthew's gospel, Jesus makes very clear where we can look to find his living presence still today: within the lives of the least of these among us. GLBT persons who hunger for God but find themselves viewed as unacceptable by the church can know this much: Christ has promised to be in their midst.

(5) Quite apart from the texts that purportedly judge homosexuality, the Bible offers a wealth of positive imagery by which to gauge the goodness of intimate relationship. Specifically, I would argue that the Bible suggests that God hopes our sexual lives will be characterized by mercy and justice, by fidelity and companionship, by a procreative spirit, and by joyful abandon. I see no reason to assume that heterosexual relationships always display these features—or that homosexual relationship never display them. Hence, it seems to me if we intend to discern the merit of any particular relationship we need to look elsewhere than at physical anatomy.

(6) Finally, for me this is finally a very personal issue. Over my 25 years as an adult I have known dozens of gay, lesbian, bisexual, and transgender

persons. And I have experienced the very graciousness of God reaching out to me through them too many times to believe that they live under God's judgment. Peter found the courage to set aside the Scripture passages that seemed to command circumcision when he saw the Spirit alive and well in uncircumcised Gentiles. Well, I have seen—again and again and again—the Spirit alive and well in the lives of non-heterosexual persons. So I can no longer believe that God dwells only on "my side of the tracks."

In the midst of my own work on their behalf, I have learned—as never before in my life—what it means, in the words of Micah 6:8 "to do justice, to practice mercy, and to walk humbly with God." I have learned this in my teaching, in my theology, in my own sexuality, and in my spirituality. In their company I have met God. For me to be less than the ally I am would be for me to sit beside Peter at the fire and to deny my friendship with Christ. I've sat by the fire often enough in my life, but on this issue I don't sit there anymore.

That's where I'm at, and why I'm there.

12. "And the Word became flesh—and pitched its tent in our midst." John 1:14
(December 2002, January 2003)

Part One

Listen, my friends, this Christmas text is *our* annunciation. This passage is *our* Red Sea parted and become dry.

I have heard many times the defensive declaration that if the Lutheran Church ever fully accepts (let alone affirms) GLBT persons it will surely split the church—because it will signify that some of us have decisively set aside the Word of God as the norm of life. Recently I have begun to see that this is a charge we should *welcome*, because it invites us to be very clear to our brothers and sisters in the church that this is precisely what we are *not* doing. We are, in fact, taking the central proclamation of the Bible with utmost seriousness, and we are passionately determined to be faithful to the Word of God. And, if we can articulate this well, we may recall enough Lutherans to the best of our tradition that, far from splitting the church, our presence will contribute to its ongoing reformation.

In the brief passage quoted above John makes two astonishing claims, and both are essential for our freedom. One has to do with "the Word," the other with "the flesh." I will consider the first claim this month and the second claim next month.

***

Bear with me for several paragraphs as I review the context for John's gospel. *We need to learn the history if we intend to know the future.*

John writes to mostly Jewish followers of Jesus. His readers are heirs to the Mosaic tradition. They revere the Torah and the Prophets as Scripture. Within this Jewish heritage they embrace Jesus as the Messiah. But they are increasingly a minority in their own tradition. For several decades after Jesus, as Jews gathered every Sabbath to worship they found themselves uncertainly side-by-side . . . some of them persuaded that Judaism found its completion in confessing Jesus as Messiah, others of them in strong disagreement.

We need a dose of humility here. Jesus was far from an obvious candidate for a messiah. Although he was clearly intent on being faithful to the Torah, he pursued this in some rather unorthodox ways, and it's really no surprise that the majority of folks in his day—and, quite honestly in ours, too—would find it unsettling to call Jesus, as a person or a pattern, "messiah": "chosen of God." If we today are not uncomfortably challenged by the inclusivity of Jesus' love, we have probably not yet paid serious enough attention to it.

At any rate, sometime around the end of the first century the tension between those Jews who embraced Jesus as Messiah and those who did not reaches a breaking point. Also, by the time this occurs something decisive has changed within Judaism: the Temple has been destroyed for perhaps 20-30 years. So long as the Temple stood, it served as the center of Jewish faith and identity. But after its destruction the Torah—Jewish Scripture—comes to stand in its place. Jewish faith finds its center in the synagogue, around the study of and fidelity to the Torah.

So finally, after years of tension, the majority of Jews—who do not accept Jesus as Messiah—decide to bar those who do. Hence, the minority, the Christian Jews are told by their brothers and sisters, "When we gather to study, to pray, to worship—to practice our faith—through the Torah, you are not welcome in the synagogue." And, because household copies of the Torah are unknown at this point, to be barred from the synagogue is, in effect, to be cut off from the Word of God.

***

Okay, now we are ready to hear what John is saying to his original readers . . . and to us today. Against the background painted above, John tells his readers, "No! You are not cut off from the Word of God!" Because finally the Word of God is not held by two stone tablets, nor on the scrolls of the Torah, but is revealed in the living person of Jesus. Thus, when John writes, "The Word became flesh and pitched its tent in our midst," he opens up a path of *deeper faithfulness* to the Word of God than any loyalty to a written text could be.

Now, I do *not* rehearse any of this background to renew John's rhetoric against our Jewish cousins for whom this gospel has often been a text of terror. I rehearse it because in the present moment we see Christians in the church calling for a faithfulness to the written word that seems to me to be *patently unchristian*. Our faithfulness as Christians, regardless of orientation or identity, is not pledged to a written text but to Living Word that has pitched its tent in our very midst. Our faithfulness, while hardly indifferent to the written text, is pledged to the Pattern of Love that played itself out in Palestine in the person of Jesus.

We interpret the written text through Jesus' life. Which is to say that we heal, even when it seems like poor timing. We feast with outcasts, even when it seems imprudent (a faithfulness that makes clear the need for *deep* solidarity among gays and lesbians—*and bisexual and transgender persons*). We touch one another in joy and justice, even when others murmur against us as though we were lepers or bleeding women. And we thrive as branches bearing fruit for a Vine that others cannot imagine nourishes our lives.

Friends, as the struggle rises, and as the charge is made that we wish to forsake the Bible, we should not evade the charge. We should reply in all earnestness, "No. Rather, we have allowed the Bible to direct us to the Word living within it . . . and leaping off its pages to dwell in our midst even today. And it is to this Living, Breathing, Loving, Surprising, Welcoming Word that we pledge our faithfulness." In making this clear to our brothers and sisters in the church, we may well remind them that our common destiny is not to be People of the Book, but People of the Word. It is a world of difference, and a difference able to change the world.

There are many fronts on which to press our welcome in the church. The Bible is not the only one, the easiest one, or (perhaps for us) the most important one. But neither is it one we need to nervously sidestep. Listen, the Word beckons to us. *See, the ground is dry. Come, cross over.*

Part Two

Last month, as Christmas approached, I considered how John's proclamation of the Incarnation of the Word expands how we understand textual authority. I suggested that in John's words *the biblical text eclipses its own authority*. John invites—or perhaps demands—of his readers devotion not to a textual word but to a tactile Word, not to inspired letters but to enfleshed Love. This does not demean the text but simply states the matter most honestly: the words on the page are like still photos of a living—and lively—God who can be best glimpsed *in action* in the surprising and subversive ministry of Jesus.

I also suggested that John's declaration about the Word become flesh has just as much to say about how we understand *our* flesh. Like the once popular graffiti message, "Kilroy was here," the mystery of the Incarnation scribbles on *our flesh* the message "God was here"—or, more accurately given John's rich sacramental theology, "God *is* here."

***

Again, we need to review some context for John's gospel back then if we wish to reclaim its power for right now. Besides being written against the backdrop of Jewish-Christian tensions, John's gospel responds to Gnostic assumptions. Gnosticism is not really a distinct religion or philosophy. Rather, it is a collection of assumptions that, like a virus, can infect a host and utilize the host as a means for replicating itself. Gnostic tendencies were widespread in many religious and philosophical traditions in the latter part of the first century.

Gnosticism takes it name from the Greek word *gnosis*, meaning "knowledge," and one of its defining elements is the promise of offering knowledge hidden to others. But a second Gnostic feature is more relevant to us here. This is the claim that there is a fundamental opposition between spirit and matter, between God and creation. From a Gnostic perspective, God is *pure* spirit; hence the physical world is *precisely where God is not*. Because God is perfect, the imperfect world of change—of aging and disease, and, yes, of passion—is a world where God *cannot* be. Thus, Gnosticism, through whatever host tradition it distorted, promised secret knowledge that would allow one to escape the pitfalls and ultimately the very fact of material existence in favor of another plane altogether. (The Heaven's Gate cult of several years back was a contemporary Gnostic tradition.) In Gnosticism the physical world is *not* God's creation; it is the obstacle to be overcome—denied and cast off—in order to find God.

***

Let's return to John's gospel. Starting in 1:1-3 John gives God *credit* for creation through the Word. Here the physical world, far from being in opposition to God, stands in *loving relationship* with God (3:16). And far from being a place where God would never dwell, it becomes precisely *the place where God chooses to dwell*, to "pitch a tent" in the original Hebraic expression. John's astounding claim, in a world rampant with Gnostic influence, is that far from despising flesh, *the Word became flesh.*

God found the human body a worthy place to dwell. Worthy enough, indeed, that we might hear in John's words the intuition that bodies, like bushes, can burn with divine presence without being consumed. And what this suggests about interpreting our bodies is no less important than what it suggests about interpreting the written text.

The body has the capacity to bear the Word. And it (like the written text) can be discerned as bearing the Word insofar as it resonates with the lived Word incarnate in Jesus. In other words, as often as my own callused feet carry me into situations where I promote liberation, understanding, and reconciliation, *God is here.* As often as my own body is given to consorting with outcasts, welcoming children, feeding those who hunger, or healing those who ache, *God is here.* And as often as the spine-tingling delight (or mundane release) of lovemaking is leavened by a love that truly honors the other, then, too, *God is here.* To say "the Word became flesh" is to say that God invites us to discover in our own bodies a hint of the holy.

John's text suggests that while sin surely distorts the landscapes of our lives, God's creative zeal has not been thwarted . . . and wherever and whenever human lives bear this Word of Love into birth again, God whispers with fresh delight that primordial word of creation, "Ah, how very good."

Last month I argued that the Incarnation invites us to adopt a hermeneutic (an interpretive principle) that reads the entire biblical text through the lived ministry of Jesus. This month I want to add that it also declares God's willingness to make a human body the locus of divine presence and revelation.

Listen carefully: the narratives of our own lives—both our experiences of exile and rejection as well as our experiences of welcome and reconciliation are also *inspired texts. Our lives, too, are lived within the Breath of God.* As the ELCA wrestles with sexuality we will need the courage to speak our own texts as articulately and passionately as we encounter the canonized texts. When the Word became flesh, the Word invited our flesh to find words and to speak in its own voice. It is time to lift this voice with as much clarity and confidence as possible.

Let me speak plainly for a moment as a straight man talking to my GLBT kin. What I have said in this essay about human flesh bearing divine presence, this is something your straight brothers and sisters know even less than you do. I am convinced that the vast majority of straight Christians are *sexual Gnostics*—that is, we cannot imagine our sexuality as a facet of our humanness that God would dare to dwell in. We say the words, "Sexuality is one of God's good gifts," but we silently editorialize to ourselves, "Yeah, right—that sure ain't the way I learned it growing up." So we have basically ignored any link between our sexuality and our spirituality—successfully (after all, we're not condemned on account of our straight sexuality). So we confess that in Jesus "the Word became flesh," adding *"but surely not below the waist!"* without ever really embracing the radicalness of that claim for ourselves or for others.

I do not presume that all GLBT persons have their spirituality and sexuality in perfect harmony, but one of the ironies of your oppression on account of your sexuality is that your very choice to persevere in your spirituality while also affirming your sexuality (even if with deep ambivalence) means that you at least have begun the conversation among yourselves that most straight Christians haven't even imagined yet. And if there is one insight

I can bring to you as a straight man it is this: much (maybe most) straight discomfort with non-straight sexuality is simply the projection onto you of a fundamental discomfort with being in our own skin. We have yet to learn for ourselves what it means to say, not just of Jesus but also of ourselves, that the Word longs to become flesh . . . even in our own bodies.

It is hardly your job to help us, but here is a mystery: *your liberation in the body politic of the ELCA waits upon the liberation of a sufficient number of straight persons in their own bodies sexual.* If you dare to help us learn how to speak of these things for ourselves, I dare say you will also empower many of my straight brothers and sisters to become the allies you need them to be.

The Word has become flesh. *May these be days in which our flesh finds the words to become the Word in our midst again.*

This essay, originally written for the Lutherans Concerned/Twin Cities newsletter, reflects on the decision of Bishop Peter Rogness to lift the sanctions imposed earlier by Bishop Mark Hanson on St. Paul-Reformation Lutheran Church for their extraordinary ordination of Pastor Anita Hill. While applauding the Bishop's decision, I also raise questions about the words in which he couched it.

13. Is "the wisdom of Gamaliel" Enough?
(January 19, 2003)

No, of course not. But I'll come back to that. Let me begin with my friend, Maria. Years ago she told me she was adopted and explained that her parents had raised her with this knowledge from the very start. "So, you see," she said, "I've had a lifelong sense of 'not-knowing.' I've lived my whole life knowing how little I actually know of my own life at its very source. I live each day with the awareness that I am tethered to persons unknown to me." Think about that.

On January 15th, Bishop Peter Rogness of the Saint Paul Area Synod lifted the sanctions that his predecessor, Bishop Mark Hanson, had imposed on St. Paul-Reformation (SPR) for the ordination of Anita Hill. The sanctions had barred SPR's pastors or members from serving on synod- or conference-level committees or task forces. In other words, for having broken the rules, the congregation was placed in an institutional "time-out."

Rogness acted in response to a resolution from his Synod Assembly last April, but knowing that his decision is sure to be controversial, he announced it through a carefully-worded statement in which he recalled "the wisdom of Gamaliel," commending the memory of this early Jewish leader to members of the ELCA today. In the earliest days of the church, when the entire movement was just a splinter group within the Jewish tradition, the Jewish high council arrested the apostles and considered simply killing them all. Gamaliel, a member of the council, cautioned them, advising, "If their (the apostles') actions are merely of human origin they will fail of their own accord, but if their actions are of God, you will not be able to stop them—and you may find yourselves fighting against God!" (Acts 5:38-39)

57

However subtly, Rogness has dared to suggest that *perhaps* by imposing sanctions on churches like SPR that, as he puts, "have pressed the edges of our pattern of life together," the ELCA has unwittingly been "fighting against God." Subtle or not, this is no small observation. True, Rogness also notes that SPR remains in violation of this ELCA policy and under admonishment because of that. But his decision offers something far more hopeful than simply looking the other way. While asserting that his decision to end the sanctions "is not intended to bias or influence" the ongoing ELCA study process concerning homosexuality and the ordination of homosexual persons, it cannot help but have an impact. And in my view that impact is largely for the better. *Largely.*

The bishop's decision is hopeful—*very hopeful indeed.* But it is not without a measure of ambiguity for those persons whose spiritual and vocational lot hangs in the balance, and we need to be honest about this. The bishop comes closest to defending SPR's choice to ordain Anita in acknowledging the legitimate need for "missional leadership" in "specific contexts," and then suggesting that this may warrant some "flexibility" on the part of the church. *Is that all we want?* The logic suggests that (maybe) we can ordain persons like Anita to minister to other persons like Anita, in the same way that we ordain women to minister to women, and persons of color to minister to persons of color, and single persons to minister to the single, etc. *But we don't do that!*

The argument cannot simply be that we need to ordain persons in committed same-sex partnerships to minister to others like them. *The argument is that we ordain them because they have experienced the call of God to minister to the WHOLE people of God and we want it to be possible for the church to affirm that call.*

My wife and I were the first straight couple that Anita married after her ordination. She led us through weeks of very fruitful premarital counseling, helping us reflect on the challenges of blending our households and families, first across the miles of a long-distance relationship and then into the space of a common home. We asked her to accompany us in this journey, not because we fit into the "specific context" for which her "missional leadership" is granted but because we saw in Anita a minister marked by warmth and wisdom and ordained to serve the whole people of God.

It is neither helpful nor wise to frame the issue as a matter of ordaining certain persons to minister to their own kind. There is only one "kind" of person in the church—sinners who have been reconciled to God. While pastors like Anita, or Ruth, or Jeff, or Phyllis, or Craig, or Donna . . . may have particular credibility with and gifts for ministering to others who have been marginalized on account of their sexuality, to ever circumscribe their ministry to those persons implies a limited, second-class status to their ordination. Perhaps worse, *it implies essential chasms between the various people of God*, as though, after 2000 years, it really *is* the case that there are Jews and Greeks, slave and free, men and women, . . . gay and straight. *Not in the eyes of God!* And I weary of defending extraordinary ordinations as though it were so.

While I recognize the strategic merit (on our part) and the ecclesiastical merit (on the bishop's part) of using "mission context" as a wedge in the struggle, I remain doubtful that it is a wedge that will open the space we really need to open. We may ultimately find that it has simply opened up a room we didn't want to be in after all. If the bishop's remarks push the larger conversation into that room, we will need to invest our energy in getting out of it.

And yet, "largely for the better" is still largely *for the better*. Because while this "wisdom of Gamaliel" solves nothing by itself, and while talk of mission context seems to me an unwise route across the Red Sea, the bishop's decision is a real opportunity. And we should seize it with zeal.

Overall Bishop Rogness recognizes that the real issue is not the ordination rule itself but the deeper question of how the church understands homosexuality (and, I would add, sexuality, period). And to study and discuss this issue while sanctioning those persons who have challenged the traditional view is itself to distort the process of study and discussion. It mutes the possibility of hearing anything new in a faith built upon the conviction that God occasionally acts in new and utterly surprising ways.

To state the matter more bluntly, leaving the sanctions in place would presume *either* that the ELCA already knows the outcome of the study (which it does not) *or* that even if the outcome favors SPR, it should have obeyed the institutional rules rather than to have followed the call of God. That last option, which all too often carries the day unspoken in most churches, hardly passes for good theology when spelled-out with stark clarity. The purpose of churches is not to pledge fidelity to institutional bylaws, no matter how nice that might be for good order; *it is to practice faithful discipleship.*

The real gift of the bishop's decision is that lifting the sanctions creates more and safer space in which study and discussion can occur. The bishop uses the language of "mutual commitment" and "mutual accountability," and in so doing he makes room for a more honest discernment of what constitutes discipleship in the realm of sexuality.

If the ELCA is to reach any deep-rooted spirit of welcome toward the GLBT persons (already!) in its midst, two things will be required: a genuine openness to the movement of the Spirit by all parties and a genuine willingness to listen to those sitting in the next pew or the next parish. Yes, there are texts to be tested, but *much more than this, there are stories to be told, fears to be named, and joys to be uttered.* And the listening must abound on all sides. We cannot guarantee this by others, but we can model it ourselves. We will need to do our share of telling, but we will also need to listen while those who fear our welcome tell the stories that anchor their fears. I do not mean the tirades or the attacks, but the honest stories.

Only in this holy space, mutually committed and mutually accountable, is discernment likely to follow the Spirit's lure toward wholeness. Which brings me (finally!) back to Maria. Bishop Rogness seems to have understood precisely her insight: *we are all tethered to persons unknown to us.* The church gains little by actions that keep us unknown to one another. It gains much by actions that dare to invite us to speak the truth of our lives, to those unknown others, to whom we are truly tethered. In this regard, the wisdom of Gamaliel is only the beginning. It is the courage of each one of us that will ultimately make the difference.

14. Threatened with Resurrection
(May 2003)

After 1700 years of Constantinian Christianity, that ungainly partnership between the gospel of Jesus Christ and the power of empire, it can be difficult to remember the deep uncertainty of that original Easter season. Moving from the fear and despair after the crucifixion into . . . who knew what?

To borrow an evocative phrase from poet Julia Esquivel, the church found itself "threatened with resurrection." And not just with the resurrection of Jesus, but with *the resurrection of the church.*

Resurrection places an unmistakable stamp of divine affirmation on the very ministry that got Jesus killed. It makes frightfully clear what it means to be a follower of "the Way." It means striving after that same radically inclusive vision and practiced solidarity in one's own life, both individually and communally. It means working to bring the church's policy toward partnered gay and lesbian pastors into line with that vision.

No wonder that, apart from the Spirit's inrushing at Pentecost, Easter remains, to this day, a season of original uncertainty for the church. Resurrection is not for the faint of heart. Confessing the resurrection, imaging Jesus' life, originally risked setting oneself at odds with the powers that be, both cultural and political. Since Constantine ushered the church into the corridors of power, confessing the resurrection has risked clashing with ecclesial powers as well. Not always, to be sure, but often enough.

What is truly remarkable, then—to the point that "miracle" is not overstatement—is that in the season after Pentecost the church *did* indeed embrace resurrection. And not merely as a claim about Jesus, *but fundamentally as a pattern in its own life.*

Many in the church today are threatened by the prospect of partnered gay and lesbian persons in ordained ministry. Resurrection life is so unimaginably new that it is almost always threatening, and those who work on its behalf are often viewed as subversive.

But the Sundays after Pentecost are *subversive Sundays*. They invite us to remember for ourselves and to remind the church that resurrection, really, is not so much about what happened to the body of Jesus, *but about what happens to the body of Christ.*

15. A Matter of Pride . . . A Matter of Faith
(June 16, 2003)

"Life does not need to mutilate itself in order to be holy." Simone Weil, the brilliant but short-lived French philosopher, was not thinking of sexual orientation when she penned these words. But she nonetheless expressed the hard won conviction of those persons who claim citizenship in both the queer community and the faith community.

Many of us have felt, at least in passing, the numbing grip of shame. But few of us have known the real and crushing terror of shame—learning to despise an inescapable truth about oneself. Queer people have been taught this shame with a fierceness known by few others. Particularly within communities of faith, queer persons have been told that holiness comes for them at the price of self-mutilation. Not physically, perhaps, but spiritually and psychically.

Many faith traditions now claim an "enlightened" stance, declaring that the issue isn't orientation but activity. No one is judged for "being" gay, only for acting on that orientation. The folly of this distinction becomes clear if we move the same logic to other arenas. "There's nothing wrong with 'being' left-handed . . . so long as you learn to use your right hand instead." (A lesson that my grandfather was taught by having his left arm tied to his desk at a Lutheran elementary school some eighty years ago.) "There's nothing wrong with 'being' deaf . . . so long as you learn to read my lips." "There's nothing wrong with 'being' black . . . so long as you learn to act like a white person."

It isn't hard to notice the blunt conditionality of this "acceptance" when framed in examples where prejudice has been largely (though not entirely) eclipsed. Now imagine: "There's nothing wrong with being heterosexual . . . so long as you never act on it." For most of us, that would be an impossible proposition.

We need not presume that our sexuality defines the whole of who we are to recognize the psychic and spiritual violence in a message that claims to abstain from judgment while effectively asking queer persons to sever their sexuality from the rest of who they are. With rare exception that's been the best message queer persons could expect from their faith communities. And it's a message that continues to breed shame.

So where do some queer folks find the audacity to live non-celibate lives of vibrant faith without paying the piper of shame? How do they come to share—as the creed of their own queer existence—Weil's confidence that "life does not need to mutilate itself in order to be holy"?

Well, sometimes lurking within the same sacred texts used to taunt them, they discover a deeper truth about unconditional acceptance—indeed of joyful affirmation. And they are willing to wager with their lives that these passages give a glimpse of the Divine less pressed into patterns of human prejudice.

Sometimes they uncover Weil's insight through their own persistent spiritual practice, responding to the Love that beckons them quite beyond all the human biases that accumulate within traditions. And they find themselves embraced by this Love despite all the advance warning that their journey would be fruitless.

And sometimes they realize this truth of uncanny grace in the most mundane ways. As they find themselves accepted, honored, and affirmed simply as they are, by persons around them—both queer and straight—they discern something Transcendent at work. They experience the welcome of the Universe in moments made holy without any mutilation of the mystery of themselves.

I am a witness to these wonders, a straight man privileged to walk among such friends. And I must tell you that among these persons for whom pride has become a matter of faith—and faith a matter of pride, there is something holy afoot.

16. Not Less than Pride . . . and Not Less than Faith
(June 16, 2003)

"But really, how can that be? I mean, HOW CAN THAT BE?" My friend reacted with genuine disbelief as I described gay and lesbian persons who find themselves drawn to paths of deep spirituality.

And in many ways his reaction was understandable. Gay pride and religious faith often appear as opposing forces. In many faith communities, annual June Gay Pride events are met with either righteous indignation or, at best, with awkward tolerance. And in most queer circles expressions of religious faith constitute obstacles to affirmation rather than occasions for it.

Many religious traditions (including those that have been dominant in the West) have seemed to suggest that sexuality itself does not mix well with spirituality. Our bodies, rife with tactile temptations, are simply not trustworthy companions in our desires for the Divine. Arguments ranging from the scriptural and philosophical to the anatomical and reproductive have all seemed to "prove" that if you're going to be sexually active on your spiritual journey, the only path leading to spiritual Truth is a "straight" one.

But that doesn't settle the matter for everyone. Against the weight of social prejudice, textual interpretations, religious pronouncements, and even the mutual mistrust between the queer and faith communities, some persons manage to stand—with pride and faith—in both communities.

These persons have discovered in the crucible of their own lives that expressions of sexuality other than heterosexual can manifest personal wholeness and moral integrity while also complementing and even deepening one's spiritual growth. They know this with a conviction undaunted by those who disagree. *They live this truth.*

Adrienne Rich, elegizing a team of women mountain climbers who perished together on a Russian mountain peak in 1974, describes their death-defying solidarity:

"I have never seen
my own forces so taken up and shared

and given back . . . till now
we had not touched our strength
we will not live to settle for less
we have dreamed of this all of our lives."

Her words capture as well the experience of those persons who discover the possibility of claiming Gay Pride alongside their membership in communities of faith.

So, "HOW CAN THAT BE?" The answer begins simply with the humble, if incredulous, recognition *that it is.* How does anyone ever account for the mysterious presence of Spirit in the midst of human lives? Theologians and mystics, prophets and poets, if they are wise, recall that the sheer freedom of Divine Love makes a capacity for reverent surprise the first prerequisite for those wishing to speak of the Spirit's movement. Accounting comes later, if at all (why am *I* loved, except because That which sits at the heart of the universe is Itself Love?). Acknowledgement and wonder come first.

That the twin drives of sexuality and spirituality can compete with one another is drilled into us long before adolescence presents us with the dilemma in our own flesh. But that they might instead complement one another—and do so in diverse ways, allowing us to touch a strength both rare and revolutionary—is an insight much neglected and much needed.

The political, social, and economic fractures so evident in our world today are rooted not least in our willingness to set spiritual pursuits in antagonistic relationship to bodily wholeness, most obviously for our queer brothers and sisters, but also for those of us who are straight.

Adrienne Rich, herself a lesbian, wrote of her choice to celebrate the beauty and mystery of love without waiting for the "permission" of anxious heterosexuals, "a whole new language begins here." And when that whole new language lifts its voice within a faith community, the insight it brings becomes imperative: *"we will not live to settle for less; we have dreamed of this all of our lives."*

This essay reflects—satirically—on the uproar over the decision of the Episcopalian Church to confirm, Gene Robinson, a partnered gay man, as Bishop. I had hoped it would appear as a newspaper op-ed, but several editors told me it was both too good and too hot to touch.

17. Satire: Cleaning House in the Christian Church
(August 6, 2003)

Jesus' place as titular head of the Christian Church appeared in question of late as the once-acclaimed head of the Body of Christ faced growing scrutiny from his own followers. New charges alleging questionable conduct by Jesus and certain other close associates have snowballed in recent weeks, leading some pundits to wonder aloud whether the events of the past summer will cancel the coming Christmas holiday altogether, although one prominent conservative commentator added quickly, "Not the shopping, of course!"

Inside observers suggest that the recent confirmation of an openly gay priest as Bishop in the Episcopal Church has spurred other denominations into a fit of moral housecleaning with the result that Christians worldwide may soon find the seat at the right hand of God unoccupied.

First the Evangelical Lutheran Church in America announced that it was disbanding its Sexuality Task Force in favor of a Circumcision Task Force. Explained one church official, "What it really came down to after the Episcopal vote is that homosexuality is just a Johnny-come-lately on the whole issue of extending Jesus' purported sprit of inclusion to persons of questionable character. If you trace it all the way back it really begins with St. Paul's highly dubious decision to welcome uncircumcised Gentiles into the Church."

Acknowledging that no exact figures were available, the unnamed ELCA spokesperson noted that current cultural trends regarding circumcision suggest that the ELCA has at least as many uncircumcised candidates for ministry as homosexual ones. When pressed he admitted that "probably a good number" of uncircumcised pastors are already preaching and presiding over the sacraments in ELCA parishes. The spokesperson added, "Whatever the medical arguments, circumcision is clearly a choice, and until we go back and correct our position on this we really can't address homosexuality with full credibility."

That news was met within days with an unusually swift show of ecumenical support from the Vatican's Congregation of Sacred Doctrine, which disclosed that it had recently reached a similar conclusion about St. Peter's vision of forbidden food. One Vatican priest requesting anonymity commented, "While it is understandable that Peter would make the jump from 'no kosher' to 'no cutting,' it is still regrettable that our first Pope did not foresee the Pandora's box he was opening."

The following week the Pope himself related "serious misgivings" about Jesus' choice to allow Mary to sit at his feet in Lazarus' house. Without accusing the Savior of intentional misconduct, the pontiff did say that, given first-century mores—and twenty-first-century controversy over women's ordination—Jesus' actions come precariously close to "scandal," that is, potentially leading other persons into temptation.

But nothing in the Pope's early remarks prepared listeners for his terse conclusion. Speaking slowly from a prepared text the pontiff read, "Finally, we cannot be more clear in our position that the Lord erred in ordaining women to be the first bearers of the Gospel on Easter morning. We admit that no man had ventured to the tomb so early, but inasmuch as Christ had earlier selected twelve men to be his apostles, he should have displayed more patience in waiting for one of them to behold his risen glory."

One week later, the Presbyterian Church (USA) issued a statement that, for the first time, expressed reservations about the company Jesus kept. Choosing his words very carefully, a noted Presbyterian theologian who asked not to be identified described the growing furor in his own denomination. "No one means to glibly second guess Jesus, but as scholarship reveals a more clear portrait of the 'outcasts and sinners' who comprised the Lord's following, many of them represent the very demographic—that is, the undesirables—that will only further erode the mainline church population if we seek to embrace them while also trying to respect the comfort levels of our current members."

Likewise, the United Methodist Church said it was appointing a panel of experts to review a list of "purity transgressions" that Jesus might have committed. One longtime Methodist observer reported that there has been, in recent years, "growing concern that Jesus' messianic zeal may have gotten the better of him on more than one occasion." Asked for clarification he responded, "Well, timing, for instance. Near-death healings and Sabbath miracles display a sort of 'impatient grace' that seems more concerned with community than propriety. And appearances. From prostitutes to parables, Jesus seems at times unconcerned with the scorn he appears to project for the status quo. In light of Bishop Robinson's confirmation we just think it's time to make some clear demarcations about where Jesus himself may have overstepped the later wisdom of the church."

Finally, the Southern Baptist Convention acknowledged that "Jesus sinned in his acceptance of Samaritans." In an unusually contrite tone, the SBC admitted, "For years we have thought that the Savior was too quick in his acceptance of these illegitimate pretenders to the Jewish heritage, but we have kept silent. Now we see that silence about Samaritans yesterday lends itself toward silence about same-sex relationships today. As a church we are now determined to condemn both, which compels us also to condemn Jesus." It remained unclear exactly what this meant for the future of the SBC.

Repeated attempts to reach either Jesus or God Almighty for comment were unsuccessful. But there were unconfirmed and conflicting reports from angelic sources that weeping and retching could be heard from inside the Heavenly City. One can only wonder now whether Jesus, with his apparent disregard for public opinion over his proclamation of radical grace, will quietly step aside while the church cleans house or continue his audacious efforts to build a community around so clumsy a notion as compassion.

This essay, although pretty specific in its "coming out" focus, marks a significant shift for me, because the image of body as burning bush is not specific to GLBT persons. In much of my speaking since then I have begun to develop this image of body as burning bush as one way to bring the conversation about sexuality and spirituality to the whole church. It comes from a presentation that brought me back to Luther College as a guest speaker a year after I moved to St. Paul.

18. The Body as Burning Bush: Coming Out and Other Holy Acts of Human Sexuality
(October 26, 2003)

I want to begin with a word of thanks for the invitation to be with you tonight. There are few places on this planet that are as much "home" to me as is this campus. The four years I spent teaching here were among the years of most fruitful ferment in my life. I found the courage and the affirmation to claim my gifts in these classrooms, in this chapel, in Oneota and Marty's, on the green spaces between the buildings, and in the hearts of so many students and colleagues who became friends. Thank you.

I wanted a title for my talk that would be both provocative and accurate. I think I found one: The body as burning bush: coming out and other holy acts of human sexuality. In my reflections tonight I want to offer and explore two simple claims. First, that our bodies *are* able to host the presence of God—like the burning bush that Moses stood before. And second, that human sexuality is one realm of bodily experience where God's presence can be felt—and that, therefore, there *are* "holy acts" of human sexuality, of which Coming Out is one such holy act. But I'll start with a little background.

I will draw on Christian language in my talk, not because it is the best, but because it the best that I can do. It is my faith language—and it is a language that I share with many of you. It is also, as I hope to show, a language that is more hospitable to a positive expression of sexuality than most of us have been raised to realize. But what I say tonight is not limited to Christian language as far as I can tell. The positive link between spirituality and sexuality is present in many faith traditions, and I have no reason to doubt that much of what I say as a Christian could be restated with equal conviction and insight by someone in another tradition.

70

Also, you should know that I do not speak from within the experience of being gay, lesbian, bisexual, or transgender. I speak as a straight man and an ally. Beyond this, as a poet, I have been gifted with uncommonly good ears to hear the pain and the hope of others. And I have been gifted with uncommonly good voices—many of them voices I heard right here at Luther—and they have helped me know where I, as a theologian, needed to look within the tradition to find words and images to heal wounds and to offer hope.

I also speak as a married man, and although I am the one at the podium, and I am the one who chose and crafted these words, it is only honest to say that everything I can share with you is grounded in the love that I share with my wife, Margaret. The bridge between sexuality and spirituality may be built in books, but it is only crossed in bed—and there with tenderness, love, and joy. Were it not for Margaret I'd have already exhausted any wisdom I have to share with you within these first three minutes.

Moreover, while I will admit to having a great love life, please understand that tonight I am speaking at least partly about what I can see down the road from where I'm at right now. I'm on the same pilgrimage toward sexual and spiritual wholeness as the rest of you. Maybe in moments of grace I can see further than many of you can, but don't presume I'm there yet. These are the reflections of a life still very much—and very happily—unfolding.

Since I'm here because it's Coming Out Week, my words are written with the GLBT community in mind—but they will ring no less true for those who are straight. *There are no spectators or bystanders in the audience tonight.*

***

Well, why the burning bush, for God's sake? For starters, because there are few biblical images so rich in revealing the character and purpose of God's presence in our midst.

In Exodus 3:2 we read, "and Moses looked and the bush was blazing, yet it was not consumed." The character of God's presence is such that it does not consume or destroy this world when it enters into our midst. God can dwell in a bush—or a body—without overwhelming it. Further, the burning bush is a moment of grace. God comes to Moses—and to the children of Israel groaning in slavery—not because of their great worth compared to all the peoples of the earth, but as an act of grace, as a gift. God's presence is never less than grace.

The burning bush also reveals something about the *purpose* of God's presence. The bush burns because God burns with a desire to end oppression for all people, to liberate us from whatever holds us back from true flourishing. *And* the purpose of God's presence is to *draw us into the holy acts of God.* In Exodus 3:3 we read, "Then Moses said, 'I must turn aside and see this wonder.'" But Moses' turning aside does not end with his curiosity satisfied; it ends with his people set free. Because God's presence is about grace and liberation, and about our own participation in the holy acts of God.

So the burning bush is a powerful symbol of God's presence. But the *body* as burning bush? Yes. Because, to move from simple metaphor to theological language for a moment, *incarnation includes all of us.* The miracle of Spirit taking on flesh may happen with unique power in the person of Jesus, but we all "live and move and have our being" within God who longs also to be incarnate within us.

You see, against the temptation of a dualism that sets the created world in eternal opposition to God, the best of the Christian tradition has seen creation—both bushes and bodies—as existing with the creating and incarnating activity of God. Creation is ongoing. The Bible offers two creation narratives that set the origins of the universe and the ecology of this planet within the meaning and intention of God, but creation is not something God did once and then moved on to other divine pursuits. We call God Creator not to acknowledge past deeds but to name part of God's persisting agenda. God is as active as ever still creating today. And still today, God looks on the fruit of each day's divine activity—including the fashioning and unfolding of our bodies—and calls it "good."

Clearly, humans are broken, distorted, misshapen, by the tangled cords of sins that warp our lives. We are all too capable of investing our bodies—sexually and otherwise—in deeds and desires that are destructive to ourselves and others. We gain nothing and risk much by denying this. But listen, because we have not heard this very well: *our brokenness cannot tear us from*

72

the web of creation. Misshapen as we are, even in our rebelliousness, *we bear within our bodies the possibility, the promise, of divine presence*—because incarnation is the song that God chooses to sing from the first to the last, from the height to the depth of creation.

So the body, no less than the bush, can burn with God's presence. And therefore the burning bush can offer us some insightful and empowering ways to think about God's presence within the mystery of human sexuality. This is to do Body Theology. It is to see the body—in ecstasy, in pain, and in mundane moments—as potentially revelatory, potentially sacramental, as capable of bearing witness to the presence of God without being consumed.

I have been introduced to Body Theology by women and by GLBT persons. Few of us grow up trusting our bodies enough to do body theology naturally, but straight white men have perhaps had the least reason to even consider it. In our faith tradition, revelation has usually been understood to come through the biblical text, and straight (more-or-less) white men have tended to be the authors and interpreters of that text.

So the body, perhaps because it was too democratic an arena, or too unpredictable in its longings, came to be regarded with mistrust. And the result was that texts, held by a powerful few, determined theology for many. But of late, women and GLBT persons, for whom the body—especially in its sexuality—has been a source of judgment and alienation, have begun to reclaim the body as an arena of revelation, a ground of God's gracious presence.

Thus, I choose to speak of the body—even in its sexuality—as burning bush. And thus, I claim the potential holiness of acts of human sexuality. I want to spend the rest of my time reflecting on several particular acts or moments of divine presence within our sexual experience. Moments when God dwells in the fleshy fabric of our being—like a burning bush—without consuming us but rather bearing grace, liberation, and luring us into hope. I will consider four particular moments: Coming Out, Keeping Faith, Making Love, and Giving Life.

Coming Out

This moment involves the power of naming. Human cultures have sometimes understood this power as the power to control. To call a tree "lumber" or a cow "food" is to claim a sort of control over what you can name. To call the First Americans "Indians"—to read Columbus' mistaken sense of place onto their identity—is to claim a sort of control over them. But in the Bible naming is not about power; it is about recognizing the terms of relationship. It is about establishing the identities that are necessary for relationships, for intimacy, to unfold. Adam names the creatures in the garden because God has seen that Adam is lonely, and God has created the animals not for Adam's use but for relationship. Naming begins that process; it is the first step toward final intimacy. Isaac is named "laughter" because how can his parents begin to relate to him without stating each time they call to him the wondrous humor that he is at all? Jesus is described as "Emmanuel, God-with-us" because how can one begin to relate to this man without acknowledging the God-presence in his life?

And at the burning bush Moses asks of the flames, "Who are you?" And God gives the divine name, Yahweh, as a way of setting the terms of relationship. God says, in effect, "Yes, Moses, I will tell you my name, because only knowing my name will you know how to relate to me. So, Moses, here it is: 'I WILL BE WHO I WILL BE.' Build a box for me, and it will be too small. Build a house for me, and I will exceed it. Think Pharaoh and his armies are too much for me, and I will prove otherwise. Try to limit my love to narrow doctrines or literal texts and I will burst them asunder. Because this, Moses, is my name: 'I WILL BE WHO I WILL BE.' I am the freedom to love and liberate. So long as you know that, we'll have a wonderful relationship."

The burning bush is God's moment of Coming Out. It is God's moment of claiming the identity that must be known if an authentic relationship with God is to follow.

From the Original Garden to the Burning Bush, God has intended that names be doorways into relationships. And, for better or worse, they are. Call a woman a "dyke" and you've set the terms of relationship. Call a man a "fag" and you've set the terms of relationship. Call someone a "pervert" and you've set the terms of relationship. Given the way that names can shut down relationships, it is good that Lutherans insist that one of the first names we receive, given to everyone at the baptismal font, is "child of God." That, too, sets the terms of relationship and these are terms much more likely to blossom into the intimacy that God hopes will crown relationships the way Sabbath crowns creation.

In this sense, coming out, naming one of the deep fundamental truths about yourself, describing one pattern in the fabric that comprises your identity and sets the terms for those who wish to be in relationship with you, is not unique to sexuality or to GLBT persons. For me to name myself a poet after having walked for years in the direction of "professor" was a coming out experience. For me to name myself a heterosexual man without shame in the presence of God and those around me is a coming out. For me to name myself an ally of GLBT persons is a coming out. *Because each act is a step toward the honesty that is the first requirement of real intimacy.*

But this isn't about me tonight. So, those of you who are gay, lesbian, bisexual, or transgender, listen up. Know this: *the moment that you dare to say with sheer honesty, this is my name, this is who I am, and I am this person with the blessing of God—in that moment you burst full into flame with the presence of God.*

In naming yourself with honesty, in claiming (even in desperation) the blessing of God, you make this naming a moment of deep grace. You make this truth a gift, both to yourself and to others. In this moment you are able to feel, even if framed by the fear fed by church and society, the glimmer of liberation *from* isolation and alienation and *for* relationship and intimacy. Because God invites you into this moment *not* to consume you but to display the beauty of who you are to the world, to lure others into saying, "Let me turn aside to see this wonder." And to *lure you* into the hope of a life filled with more holy acts, with more moments of grace and liberation. *In the moment of Coming Out, you are the burning bush.*

Keeping Faith

Coming Out is seldom simple or easy. And it's usually a life-long process, because the closet keeps chasing after you as societal assumptions try to erase you again and again. The moment of coming out will need to occur again and again. So to move beyond Coming Out is not to put it behind you; it's simply to add another act to the repertoire of holiness in your life, what I'm calling the act of Keeping Faith.

When I say that Coming Out is an act of holiness I am making a blunt theological statement. I am saying that in addition to whatever *human* presence you choose for your coming out, there is also—and most fundamentally—a *divine* presence. Whether you come out to friend or family, to pastor or teacher, you come out foremost to God, because you dare to stand naked in the garden without shame.

Keeping faith, then, is about relating to others in a way that honors the divine presence at your coming out. It is about sexual ethics, and it has less to do with rules than with relationships. Keeping rules is not a holy act, keeping faith with your name and the name of God and the name of those around you—*that* is a holy act.

Sin is real. Whether you explain it by reference to a biblical fall or see it as the evolutionary baggage of our climb upward from a more brutal past, there is simply no use in denying that from the moment of our birth—or even before—we are exposed to forces that bend us into habits that are hurtful. We carry in ourselves, straight or gay, sexually active or celibate, transgender or bisexual, the weight of distorted impulses and hungers that we are taught to meet with a taste for intimacy that is rarely intimate and more often oppressive. Whether you employ the word "sin" or not, there can be little argument that our best intentions seldom find the shortest line between two points.

Keeping faith, then, is about recognizing the potential for misuse of our sexual selves—but more importantly about recognizing the potential for moments of incarnation through our sexual selves. And I say "more importantly" not to be naïvely optimistic about this, but because this other side, this potential for incarnation, has been all but lost to us in our faith tradition. We have heard, explicitly and implicitly and through the subtlety of a silence that can deafen, that our sexual bodies can betray us. But we have too rarely heard that they can course with the gracious presence of God. And in the absence of that message, the best we have been able to hope for is a sexuality that is obedient to rules—while dwelling in bodies that hunger for grace. So the "more importantly" deserves the spotlight right now: *keeping faith is about learning what you need to know so that sexuality can blossom in intimacy and incarnation rather than wither in alienation and hurt.*

This is surprisingly short and sweet. In Hebrew, the verb "to know" can also mean "to make love." So one way to frame the challenge of sexual ethics is to ask about the challenge of knowing well. And within the prophetic tradition and within Jesus' ministry we learn again and again what it means to know God well. Throughout the Bible knowing God well looks like this: justice—especially for the most vulnerable among us. It means, in the familiar words of Micah, "to do justice, to show mercy, and to walk humbly with God." That's not a bad foundation for sexual ethics. I'd say it's a pretty solid one.

Keeping faith means living out of the presence of God that marked your coming out. And if the presence of that God is known by justice, mercy, and humility, then appropriate sexual knowing—expressions of sexual intimacy that keep faith with *this* God—must pass the measure of justice and mercy. Sexual intimacy must not be exploitive of power differences, whether based in money, age, race, gender, or social role. For *any* sexual intimacy (straight or otherwise) to be ethical it must *not* transgress justice; it *must* embody mercy as the compassionate nurture of the other.

I think this implies fidelity. Sexual intimacy is among the deepest expressions of self-vulnerability that we can engage in. To do so outside the context of genuine, promised fidelity is neither wise nor safe. It carries us to the precipice of psychic, emotional, and even physical destructiveness. On the other hand, to offer and to receive such vulnerability in the midst of fidelity is truly to stand on holy ground. I do not think this means that from our first date we need to pledge strict fidelity. I *do* think it suggests that as the level of physical intimacy in a relationship rises, it must be met with an equal increase in professed—and *practiced*—fidelity.

And what does "walking humbly with God" mean in reference to sexual ethics? I think it means that the truth of being a child of God does not lie in a frenzied rush into sexual activity with the advent of adolescence, the exhilarating rush of hormones, or even with the authentic joy of coming out. Coming out does *not* mean that you need to prove yourself through sexual adventures. It does mean that you are now *ready* to know yourself, to know others, and to be known.

Let's be clear. I am *not* advocating abstinence; I'm advocating *integrity*. The grace and the liberation and the lure of keeping faith lie in this: that we live into our sexuality with patience as well as passion. That we remember that the erotic energy harbored in *human* touch is the spark of *divine* presence. The human body is holy ground. That doesn't make it off limits. It does mean we venture onto it with reverence and with wonder.

A side note here. Keeping faith is about learning to *flourish* as sexual selves. And sexuality has the unhappy distinction of being a fundamental human activity that is learned—in our society—with virtually no genuine guidance offered or sought across generations. We would all keep faith better if we knew how to talk more casually about the mundane and mysterious character of our bodies and the sexual energy that dwells in them. We can't even imagine that yet, but we won't get there magically or all at once. We'll get there by risking awkward conversations until casual conversations come more easily, and by knowing that sometimes even words of quiet counsel can be the mark of a bush ablaze with grace.

Making Love

Claiming the goodness of sexuality is not about hopping into bed as soon as possible with a clean conscience. It is, as I have tried to suggest, first and foremost about Coming Out and Keeping Faith—and learning to sense the gracious presence of God in these moments.

However, if sexuality is indeed good—if God can say, over a pair of entwined bodies, replete with the salty sweet sweat of a well-won climax, "*That* was very good"—then within the moment of faith well-kept, shaped by intimacy that is just and kind, patient and passionate, *making love is a holy act*.

Making love is not about the details of how your anatomy matches up and meshes with your partner's. It is about how you and your partner's anatomy together become mutually engaged in a crescendo of intimacy with each other's soul. And it is another moment when bodies burn like bushes, without being consumed, but bearing forth the presence of God.

I said earlier that the burning bush is a moment in which God's presence is revealed as grace, as gift. In making love we participate in this presence, becoming wholly and graciously present to another. In this moment of finding ourselves held and touched by another's love to the point of body-trembling ecstasy we come to know something *in our bodies and in our souls* of the truth of God's astonishing love—and we have been fools to blind ourselves to this by shame.

If the purpose of God's presence is to liberate and to lure us into liberating activity, then making love also participates in the purpose of God's presence. We live most of our lives hemmed in by a sense of self that ends where our skin stops, but in lovemaking we find ourselves drawn into the hungry awareness that selves find their ecstatic completion in this other who is just beyond where I thought my mere self stopped. This is surely a wonder that must be seen.

But there is one more moment beyond this. Because *finally we make love—like burning bushes—not simply to savor ourselves but to be drawn into God's yearning to save the world.*

Giving Life

Liberation, in Exodus, is not just personal or interpersonal; it is full blown society-shaking liberation. And I am ready to say that when lovemaking is allowed to burst into full flame with the presence of God it can have society-shaking consequences. In my own body's ecstasy I get one glimpse of what it means for *this* body to be fully alive. In my happy privilege to bring Margaret's body to ecstasy, I come to realize that I am able to participate deeply and wonderfully in the flourishing of *another* body. And in these twin perceptions, sustained by the presence of God, a power is released that is no longer specifically sexual but which bears in it the hope that *all bodies* might flourish. A hope that makes my personal ecstasy the measure of my highest ideals. How can I know this deep joy in my body and not make it my lived hope that other bodies cease to know hunger, poverty, war, fear?

79

Thus, I will say that sexuality is indeed intended to be procreative, to give life; but our own prejudice—perhaps our desire to stem the flow of God's creative energy into the world—has led us to understand this in a narrow, biological fashion. But truly, to find ourselves partnered in longing love with another person is to find that we have company in the work of caring for creation. Whether you are gay, lesbian, bisexual, transgender, or straight—whether you are celibate or sexually active, single or in a relationship—one truth that we hear in the biblical creation account is that human beings were created to tend the Garden, to guide creation's bounty and to tend its scarcity in ways that promote the flourishing of all. That's *why* we're here. The joy that we know sexually in our bodies is there, at least in part, to lure us into the holy act of caring for all that is embodied, for all the ecological diversity that reflects God's rampant desire for incarnation.

We don't need a partner to do this. But if in our partnerships we fail to look outward and tend to the corner of creation around us—whether that is children or other humans, animals or ecosystems, or simply our household resources—if our love for another person does not spill out into these areas, we have missed something of the presence of God. God is always engaged in the care of life, especially among the vulnerable. And no one need shrink from the expectation that Christian sexual love should be procreative. *Lived well, it always is.* And here, too, the bush burns brightly.

***

Even though it is Coming Out Week, I have focused more on the goodness, the potential holiness of sexuality *per se* rather than on the acceptability of a GLBT identity. I've done this for a couple of reasons. Let me conclude by explaining why.

I hope that my words have offered insight and empowerment to those of you who are GLBT, whether you're out already or still on your way. Everything I've said has been intended to invite you to embrace with joy and integrity the gift of who you are. Yet the oppression that you face will not be erased simply by your insight and empowerment. Justice, as Martin Luther King, Jr., recognized, is a seamless garment. The generations of sexual and spiritual injustice toward GLBT persons have inevitably distorted sexuality and spirituality for all of us. *Your* liberation and *my* liberation go hand-in-hand. Not because I have suffered as much or waited as long, but because until we who are straight can be freed from the fear of our own sexual energy—a fear that drives us to fear you and your sexual energy even more deeply—until liberation comes for *all* of us, wounds will continue to afflict far too many of you. So my words have tried to push that liberation along for everyone.

Second, the question of whether you who are gay, lesbian, bisexual, or transgender are acceptable in the eyes of God, the argument over whether your lives and your love can be justified does not hold my interest much any longer. Yes, there are texts and traditions to sort through. There are sincere and profound convictions on both sides of the matter. But I am transfixed by the words of that Presence that leaps in tongues of flame from the burning bush. That Presence says, "I will bring liberation to my children. I will bring them to a land where they can flourish. Because *I am the one who will be who I will be*. I am the freedom to love across human boundaries and to burst the limits of human boxes."

That same Presence is echoed in the prophetic call to do justice and love mercy and walk humbly. *You* can do these things. That same Presence is echoed in Jesus' remark that those who do good in his name are to be accorded respect even if the disciples don't recognize them as part of the regular group. *You* can do good in Jesus' name. That same Presence is echoed in Paul's determination that Gentiles are welcome in the church because God loved them regardless of circumcision or diet. God loves *you* no less than Gentiles. And that same Presence is echoed in Peter's readiness to accept Gentiles when he sees that the Spirit has been poured out on them even though their lives don't match the prescriptions of good Jewish behavior. I have seen the Spirit poured out upon some of *your* lives even while your love falls outside the prescriptions of the church.

So finally for me the texts fall silent. I have seen the holiness of God in gay, lesbian, bisexual and transgender persons. Finally for me this is not about justifying your behavior or even about how I regard the authority of a written text. It is about how I respond to the presence of a living God who has chosen to dwell in your lives as in a burning bush. I was not raised to expect this, but who I am to tell God that your lives are off limits? Who was Moses to tell God that bushes can't burn without being consumed?

God *is* present in gracious, liberating and luring ways in the mystery of our sexual lives. In coming out, in keeping faith, in making love, in giving life. We *are* bodies that can burn like bushes without being consumed. I have turned aside to see this wonder. I hope you will, too.

This poem was the centerpiece of a sermon preached for Reconciling in Christ Sunday, 2004, honoring the witness of those churches that are explicit in their welcome and affirmation of GLBT persons. The texts for the day included the conversion of St. Paul, so I wrote about Fred Phelps, the Kansas 'pastor' all too well known for his hate-filled venom for all things gay.

19. The Turning of Fred
(January 2004)

Fred's face was red and his voice was shrill
And his eyes let loose a look could kill.
"I am born and raised a child of Christ,
Birthed by my mama and by God born twice.
Zealous I am for the ways of the Lord,
For the Word of God is a two-edged sword."
With words like these Fred's voice grew strong –
With the World Wide Web his reach grew long;
With the URL "godhatesfags,"
Old Fred's fury never flags.
Believing the Bible ordained his cause,
Fred spewed venom with nary a pause.
Claiming the Word was chiseled in stone,
He narrowed the kingdom to straight alone.
When a Matthew died—by hatred fell—
Fred tallied up his days in hell.
When a lesbian pastor was stoled in red,
Fred brought signs saying here "fags wed."
When a new church voted for RIC,
Fred brought his hate for all to see.
And on it went, for months and years,
Fred breathed threats and murderous fears.
He lobbied world leaders, from time to time,
To make gay sex a capital crime.
He violently persecuted the church of God,
Convinced the Lord Himself had given him the nod.
So just like Paul, Fred was loyal to a law;
A list of do's and don't's was all Fred saw.
And there the story stands still today, my friends,
But the Gospel truth says this ain't where it ends . . .
Imagine with me—Fred driving along,

Humming the tune to a hate-filled song,
Off to bash more of the GLBT crowd,
Doing what he does in the name of God.
Doing 65 on the interstate,
This is the day that'll change Fred's fate.
Suddenly a light fills up Fred's head;
While his van drives on, Fred's as good as dead.
In the blink of an eye, from the east to the west,
Fred's whole life is put to the test.
A voice calls out, *"Fred, listen up, please!*
You are hurting Christ through the least of these."
"Who is it, pray, that speaks?" Fred cries.
"I am Jesus Christ," comes the quick reply.
"Fred, you say you're towing the gospel line,
But the folks you're damning are friends of mine.
They are sealed by my love and called by name,
And if you honor me, honor them the same.
I am the Word—and quite alive you see;
Gathering the outcast, for all are kin to me.
You persecute my followers, but this is very odd,
When you persecute them, you persecute God.
It's time to turn around, my dear friend, Fred,
There's work to be done, and you're going in my stead."
Then the voice fell silent, and the light went pale,
And from Fred's eyes fell something like scales.
And some in the van heard a sound; saw no light;
While others heard nothing but exclaimed at the bright.
Well, Fred pulled over at the next rest stop—
Broke the rules, built a fire, burned his signs right up.
"Friends," he said, to his helpers in hate,
"Like St. Augustine, I've come to love God late.
I thought that the Lord was bound by ink,
But I see now, that I failed to think.
From the first to the last, God's creative role
Is to mend the world, and make it whole.
God isn't a judge who sits above;
God simply yearns to see us love."
With the signs turned to ashes and his heart on fire,
Fred could hardly wait to send it out on the wire.

If you go to "godhatesfags" now, this is what you'll see:
"This site has moved—'cause God spoke to me.
You'll be redirected quickly; note the name change, please,
Now entering the site: 'God *loves* GLBT's!'"

Now that's a fanciful tale, playfully told,
But mark my words as I make them bold.
The limit to the tale is the limit to God,
And to limit the "I AM" would be pretty odd.
So it just might happen, just like I said,
Someday soon when God turns Fred,
But a good news story is only good and new
If it reaches out and grabs a hold of *you*.
So the real question isn't about Fred or even Paul;
It's, How will *you* answer the good news call?
There's work to do a'plenty to make welcome in the pew,
And the workers in the harvest are always far too few.
It's reconciling time—the year of Jubilee—
When the Lord bids come *all* of you and me.
Can you hear the Word of Welcome, taking on flesh and bone?
'Tis the mystery of Christ that his voice . . . *is your own*.
The welcome of God—listen well, my friend—
Is the very human welcome that *you* extend.
In your reconciling life—as you worship, as you live—
The presence of God is the gift that *you* give.
It may cost you a little; it may cost you a lot;
'Cause the church and the world would rather welcome not.
But the Spirit blows free, and God's love reaches far
And the door to the Kingdom is always left ajar,
So the challenge is make the people of God whole,
And by your endurance you will gain your soul.

This essay offers a critique of the ELCA's 2003 sexuality study. It appeared in the March 2004 issue of the Lutheran Concerned/Twin Cities newsletter.

20. A Journey of Questionable Merit
(February 20, 2004)

When I set out to review *Journey Together Faithfully, Part Two: The Church and Homosexuality (JTF2)* I tried to be thorough and found myself being pathetically dry instead. I tried to be upbeat and found myself sounding hopeful in a very strained sort of way. So I will just get to the point. This study is mediocre in a moment when the church can ill afford mediocrity. It is not terribly offensive, just quietly disappointing. And not because it is "balanced," but because it seems almost determined (despite its lofty aims) to remain banal.

Before I tell you why *JTF2* is such a disappointment, let me urge you to still make the most of the opportunity it does present in the church. Actively participate in your church's study of it—and look for every opportunity to tell a story rather than talk about an abstract idea. Urge your church to supplement the study by viewing "This Obedience" (the story of the ordination of Anita Hill) and perhaps "What Do You Say When Someone You Love Says, 'I'm Gay'?" (a short video featuring Bishop Emeritus Paul Egertson relating the journey toward his acceptance and celebration of his gay son) or "Tim and Patrick" (a short video about the blessing ceremony of a gay couple, one of them the son of Bishop Emeritus Darold Beekman). All the videos are available at www.lcna.org/infox. Bottom line: ensure that in your congregation the study of homosexuality has a human face.

As for the study itself, the single greatest shortcoming is that it aims to engage the present-day experience of ELCA members on the matter of homosexuality—and nowhere implores, adjures, or requires that churches explicitly invite and listen to the present day experience of homosexual ELCA members. Their voices are absolutely, utterly, unequivocally essential to the integrity of any conversation about their place in the church. Yet the study's relative silence on this—it goes no further than calling their participation "helpful"—allows their witness to be merely optional. Given the level of discomfort about this issue in the church, optional voices get erased.

In this respect the study fails to reckon honestly or adequately with the level of fear on both sides of this issue or with the legacy of judgment, intimidation, and covert and overt violence against homosexuals in church settings. It notes that gay and lesbian persons are already welcome in the church—per Churchwide Assembly actions—but never actually asks whether that legislative action has translated into the genuine parish-level hospitality that is the prerequisite of any faithful journey. Stories of faith—of alienation and hope, of desperation and joy, of anguish and integrity—told by gay and lesbian persons will be the breath of the Spirit in the days ahead, and this study does not go very far out of its way to make sure they're told.

Another shortcoming is the pretense of "balance" by repeatedly offering a spectrum of viewpoints held by ELCA believers. We should, of course, be aware of this range of views, but it is an illusion of "balance" when the vast majority of negative views about homosexuality are held by non-homosexuals. This is not a conversation about whether heterosexual activity is right in the eyes of God. There are no gay or lesbian ELCA voices asking whether straight people can have their unions blessed or can be both married and ordained. So the stakes of this question bear entirely upon the lives, the loves, and the vocations of gay and lesbian persons. And to claim a "fair" balance by giving equal time to all perspectives without being clear about whose life, love, and vocation is at stake is simply dishonest. We have learned enough from feminist and liberationist theology to know that there are no playing fields untilted by power. But when we talk about sex, we'd like to pretend that there are.

I recognize that conservative Lutherans do have things at stake here. Like their view of the Bible, their sense of morality, their faith in the church, or even their faith—period. But against the imperiled lives, the unblessed loves, and the ruptured calls of other human beings, these things pale in importance. I am not disdainful toward these fears, but I will not pretend they are equal in weight. They are apples and oranges. Healings and Sabbaths. And at some point the prophetic task of the church and the pastoral task of the church must come together in a clear compassionate voice and make that clear.

Because this is a church study, it's inevitable—and appropriate—that theological language creep in. But we need to be brutally honest here, even if it disappoints us. Terms like "law and gospel," "orders of creation," and, yes, even "justification," are not the vernacular of most baptized Lutherans today. And every time the study drops these terms into the conversation it acts as a subtle reminder that this is really a conversation for the specialists, or at least for those confident in their theological vocabulary. Because, if you can't keep up with these words you can't possibly assess the morality or acceptability of homosexual behavior. The study's readiness to frame matters in less than transparent theological terms serves to silence the very mundane yet spirit-filled experiences of gay and lesbian Christians who may not know what the "orders of creation" are or how "law and gospel" fit together, but know crystal clearly that God's love moves between them and their partner—if only the church would quit using its godspeak long enough to listen to the Spirit as its blows where it wills.

The study, of course, treats the obvious biblical passages: the creation accounts and the "condemnatory" texts. Yet it manages to sidestep the account in Acts of the dispute over circumcision in the early church. This may well be the most applicable and instructive biblical evidence for us to consider, but it's not there.

JTF2 discusses the biblical texts it does treat in a fair and balanced way—which is to say it blithely ignores the toll of spiritual desperation, self-immolation, and violent incitement that are the unhappy but undeniable companions of the "conservative" interpretations. However, the deeper shortcoming is that the study fails to ask what it means to call the Bible "authoritative" in a way that truly respects the biblical text as the product of sincere human desire to respond to God, but one that is equally shaped by the finite viewpoints and the cultural biases of its authors. To be honest about this is not to be disrespectful to the text. On the contrary, *to hold back from making critical judgments about these things is itself to be disrespectful toward a text that bears the Infinite only through very finite means.*

Granted, the study does attend to questions of responsible biblical interpretation, but throughout this discussion it regards the Bible as a text that will solve its own problems if we just handle it responsibly. If we simply allow Scripture to interpret Scripture, recall the literary or historical context, consider the genre, or discern the key point, we will see that the Bible is authoritative in complex but not problematic ways. *I can't buy that.* The Bible has been problematic historically for countless victims of Christian imperialism, and you can't excuse that by saying those people failed to interpret it properly. If God only meant for Joshua to initiate the slaughter of whole villages, but nobody else was supposed to copy that, that's *still* a pretty problematic order to place on the lips of God even once. *Until this church acknowledges honestly and humbly the human frailty of our holiest text it will continue to betray us.*

We have a better path. When John claimed that in Jesus the Word became flesh he asserted that in the life of Jesus—in the scandalously inclusive ministry of the messiah—the capacity of the written word to contain the breadth of God was decisively eclipsed. Jesus' ministry does not make the Bible irrelevant, but it does require that we measure these written words—as did Jesus himself—against the requirements of unconditional compassion.

Finally, as though I haven't said enough already, the study seems not to notice the legacy of sexual embarrassment and/or discomfort and/or guilt and/or shame that most straight Lutherans have been formed by in their growing years. By ignoring this, the study overlooks the way that this not only limits our ability to discuss anything related to sexuality very well—but *direly limits our ability to discuss the normative edges of sexuality without projecting and magnifying our own feelings toward them.* If we *really* mean it when we say that *in our sexuality* "We are part of God's good creation," then why do we have a study document *on sexuality* that is 50 pages long and never once openly discusses any human sexual experience?! If we did nothing but sit in small groups and read out loud, in turn, the Song of Songs in contemporary English, we would at least become uncomfortably aware of how uncomfortable we really are with the goodness of our sexuality. And then we might begin to grapple honestly with the question of how we can learn to be more gracious toward the sexuality of others.

This study, I fear, will not take us very far in that direction.

This essay, prompted by a question from a reader, expands on a pair of sentences in my earlier critique of Journey Together Faithfully: "[The study] manages to sidestep the account in Acts of the dispute over circumcision in the early church. This may well be the most applicable and instructive biblical evidence for us to consider, but it's not there." Here I explain that comment.

21. Missing the Acts of God
(March 16, 2004)

It's noteworthy that in *Journey Together Faithfully Part Two: The Church and Homosexuality* (JTF2) all of the biblical texts treated are passages that can be read to either explicitly or implicitly (e.g., the creation account) condemn same-sex sexual relationships. So the "balance" presented comes down to one side arguing that these texts are irrelevant while the other argues that they're conclusively against it. All those who favor the full inclusion of homosexuals can do is defend themselves against the way the other side wants to "attack" with these texts.

But JTF2 provides not a single text that can be read to assert the rightful place of gay and lesbian persons in the church, not a single text that reverses the roles and forces those who favor excluding them from full life in the church to take the defensive position and argue that this text is simply irrelevant. *But it is not the case that no such texts exist.* The Acts texts are one such example. And they were under consideration for inclusion in the study, but as Jim Childs told some folks at one point, "They didn't 'make the cut.'" With these texts (Acts 10 and Acts 15; and Galatians as well) the roles do reverse, because they precisely concern how the church wrestled to overcome its own theological and culture prejudice in another era. But *the Task Force chose to silence these texts; to make them unavailable to us—or to the whole church—in these discussions.* If this does not constitute a betrayal of the Task Force's very commission, it comes very close.

Let's begin in Acts 10 with Peter and Cornelius. It seems significant that Luke records Peter's vision (in which God invites, then orders Peter to feast on foods previously viewed as unclean) twice, both in Acts 10 and Acts 11. Luke seems intent on emphasizing the importance of this vision in shaping

90

the life, mission, and self-understanding of the early church. In fact, there are two central visions that animate Luke's story: this one by Peter and the vision Paul receives on the road to Damascus—also repeated twice in Acts. Both visions have to do with how the church relates to its Jewish roots. Recall that Paul is persecuting the early (at that time still Jewish) church out of his own zeal that they were betraying the fundamentals of the Jewish faith. Both visions also have to do with moving the church toward a posture of openness and welcome toward the Gentiles—a catch-all phrase for the Jews that meant basically "everyone not like us." (In the church today "gentiles" might mean "anyone who isn't straight.")

I think the key verse in the whole section is perhaps 10:44-47 where Luke records how the "proof" that the Gentiles have been welcomed by God – with no strings attached, no cutting required—was established by the outpouring of the Spirit on them *just as they were*. Peter affirms this stance in Acts 15 (vv. 8-9) and Paul and Barnabas chime in with their accounts of how they have seen first hand God's gracious and miraculous activity among the Gentiles.

For none of Peter, Paul, or Barnabas does the question of circumcision hinge on reading the word of God rightly—there would be *no way* to read the written word to allow for uncircumcised Gentiles to become believers. Rather they see that the question hinges on how they read the activity of God in their midst. And they see that God is active in places and ways that the written word could not have led them to anticipate. (James does go looking for a biblical text to help support this—Acts 15:13-18, but that's an afterthought in the text; it isn't what drives the scene.)

Even if the importance of these texts is granted, some will then focus on the "offenses" that the Gentiles are asked to avoid and suggest that same-sex activity is one such "offense" today that the church is asking homosexuals to avoid. Before going there it's worth noticing that Peter frames the whole discussion as a matter of putting God to the test. For Peter *any restrictions at all* come precariously close to undermining the claim about God's grace. For him, to require circumcision of the Gentiles (or "straight"/"celibate" behavior of gays) is not so much an affront to the Gentiles as *it is an insult to God because it challenges the core claim that God's grace is enough—period.*

So whatever "offenses" the church might want to ask gay and lesbian persons to refrain from should be made with the explicit awareness that in making such request the church is moving in the direction of putting God to the test.

Well, what *would* it mean today to avoid meat offered to idols? It might mean to avoid clothing made in sweatshops—those are the goods in our marketplace that are produced under conditions of idolatry in which profit is god. This has nothing to do with sexuality. Such a request could be made by the church to *all* its members. And the fact that it would strike most U.S. Christians as excessively "political" says something about how acceptably idolatrous our culture has become to us.

What *would* it mean today to avoid blood or strangled meats? This prohibition is grounded in the ancient Jewish belief (Lev 17:11, a passage with atrocious implications of its own in regard to atonement theology) that the life-force of a creature resides in the blood and that it would somehow misuse that life force to consume it as food. The life force was sacred. Besides a literal reading, the passage might well suggest that the church should ask homosexuals to avoid any meat that has been factory-farmed or inhumanely butchered since such processes fail to respect the sacred life force that resides in other creatures. But again, this is a prohibition that has nothing to do with sexuality, and is one that the church could make with credibility to all its members (but would never dare to).

Finally, what *would* it mean today to avoid "fornication" (NRSV)? Countryman notes that the word behind this is better rendered "harlotry," and that in its first mention (15:20) it is likely a more vivid way of prohibiting idolatry which in Leviticus (17:7) is described as "playing the harlot" in chasing after other gods. Nowhere does Leviticus (which is the source of the prohibitions against blood, idols, and strangled meat) use "harlotry" in a sense other than either idolatry or basic prostitution. So gay and lesbian persons should maybe be asked by the church to avoid idolatry and to avoid clandestine sexual encounters where money is exchanged. We might ask that of straight Christians as well. I doubt either side would balk much at this.

But, of course, people will want to read "harlotry" as "fornication" and will want to read "fornication" as condemning "illicit" sexual relations (that is, any sex that straight Christians don't like). I think we need to be honest in acknowledging that what constitutes "illicit" sex is always culturally shaped. Is "petting" fornication? At what point does it become so? Is premarital sex "fornication"? What about post-marital sex between seniors? Is oral sex? Even between straight people? Is anal sex? Even between straight people? Is mutual masturbation? What about sex while menstruating? These are all questions that would be answered differently by Christians in different times and places. There is no universal timeless Christian sexual ethic; fornication is a moving target.

So what *would* make sexual relations "illicit" today? I would argue that an absence of justice, mercy, humility, compassion, procreative impulse, and joyful abandon all make for sexual relations that fall short of God's intent. (But see the latter part of my essay on "The Bible and Homosexuality" for a fuller explanation of this—especially the way I treat "procreation.") Again, that's a basic ethical stance—shaped by our understanding of gender equality (quite foreign to the first century) and the role of sexuality in human life overall—that I think is very defensible today as a God-pleasing approach to sexual ethics, but I never could have sold it in the Middle Ages (or even in the early 20th century).

Yet part of what we have learned about sexuality over time is that it is a fundamental facet of who we are. And this does bring it into relationship with circumcision. For the Gentiles, despite their body-spirit dualism, the human body was an ideal of beauty. To be asked to circumcise the male penis was—from their perspective—a requirement that they practice male genital mutilation in order to become Christian. In fact, that's the very language Paul uses in Galatians—mutilation—because Paul sees what's at stake from their perspective (also in Phil 3:2). They're not just "trimming off the foreskin," they're being asked to *mutilate* themselves. In Galatians 5:12 Paul's rhetoric reaches a high point in saying, "I wish those who unsettle you (over the

93

"need" to be circumcised) would castrate themselves!" (NRSV) The Catholic Study Bible renders the verse like this, (paraphrased from memory by me) "I wish while these Jews were circumcising themselves that the knife might slip and cut off the whole thing!"

From this angle, Paul might argue today, "To those who wish homosexual persons to mutilate their very selves to become Christian—would that these straight people be forced to go through reparative therapy themselves!" That's how angry Paul is, because for him, as for Peter, this whole topic threatens to compromise the grace of God—a grace that he is not simply convinced of in his head but which he has seen firsthand with his own eyes traveling in the midst of the Gentiles.

Which brings me back to my fundamental critique of JTF2. *Nowhere* does it *compel* us to listen to the "signs and wonders" (Acts 15:12) that have been occurring in the lives of gay and lesbian persons who are quite "uncircumcised" by the church's standard. *Nowhere* are we *compelled* to listen to the stories of personal faith and church life renewed by their presence. *Yet this is precisely how the early church wrestled with the issue of circumcision, and the Task Force has simply erased that model from the front and center place it deserves.*

Lastly, these texts also suggest something about how we might appeal to Scripture in all of this. As I suggest elsewhere, we need to read the written Word through the life of the Living Word. Jesus' life is the embodied practice of inclusive compassion. And he uses those biblical texts that enhance inclusive compassion and challenges those biblical texts that compromise inclusive compassion. Jesus is *not* a biblical literalist; he is a compassionate prophet and messiah who sets his hermeneutical (interpretive) compass by the compassion that he sees at the heart of God (Luke 6:36). In Acts 10 and 15 we see Peter, Paul, and Barnabas all doing the same. If only the JTF2 Study has invited us to follow suit. Our conversations as a church will be poorer for having missed a chance to dwell together on what these texts tell us about the acts of God in surprising ways and unexpected places.

I developed this talk at the invitation of St. Frances Cabrini Catholic Church in Minneapolis. They were celebrating their tenth anniversary as a Welcoming parish, having drafted a public Statement of Reconciliation aimed at the GLBT community in 1994. They asked me to address the biblical texts often used to condemn homosexuality. This is NOT my favorite topic. I am not a biblical scholar, and I think there are better ways to employ our energy than dodging the assaults of others. Still, it is perhaps necessary work, and I used it as an opportunity to move beyond the texts themselves to some wider remarks about how we can more creatively—and more faithfully—approach the Bible.

22. Holding our Breath in the Face of Hate: Reading the Bible "Word by Word" in the Spirit of Christ
(October 12, 2004)

My presentation is arranged in two broad parts. In the first half I will speak directly to the biblical texts so often used to terrorize the gay community. This is the least of what I want to talk about, but it is where I will begin. In the second half, I will explain why I think simply "defusing" these few texts is not enough—why I think that we must *and can* do better. And I actually *will* do better: by suggesting what I believe is a far more faithful and promising way to approach Scripture. Finally, I will conclude with a few short reflections on what all of this means when it comes full circle to the practice of our sexuality. And afterwards I'll look forward to your comments and questions.

Let me first, however, be clear about who I am. I am *not* gay, but I have so identified myself with these people and this struggle that I sometimes speak using first person pronouns. By this I do not mean to blur the distinctions—as though this struggle is the same for me as it is for those who identify as gay, lesbian, bisexual, or transgender. *It is not.* But I will be restless in the very depths of my soul until *all of us* find a welcome in the church. I have invested my reputation, my livelihood, my scholarship, and my creativity in this struggle—without reserve. I do not speak as a bystander or an interested observer; *I speak as a co-conspirator in the remaking of the church.*

I have two Masters degrees; one in Theology from Wartburg Seminary, a Lutheran school, and one in Christian Ethics from the University of Notre Dame. I have taught college courses in GLBT Theology and have been a vocal and active ally in the Lutheran Church. And for several years I coordinated the welcoming program for Lutheran congregations in the Twin Cities. But, perhaps more than any of this, I need simply to acknowledge that my life has been leavened—enriched and transformed—by the friendship and grace I have known from GLBT persons. Lastly, while I do bring some significant learning to this presentation, I speak primarily as a poet, as someone convinced that these truths will finally be received not as ideas grasped by our minds but as images embraced by our hearts.

***

There are six of them. So few passages altogether compared to the entire text of the Bible that we might easily overlook them . . . except that they drip with blood. Surely most Christians who feel compelled to condemn homosexuality on the basis of these texts *do not* endorse violence against GLBT persons. Yet it is undeniable that the violence that does get perpetrated against this community almost always understands itself as legitimated in some way by these texts. They drip with blood whether they were meant to or not. And like a vicious pet dog that has a habit of getting out and terrorizing the neighborhood, *because these texts belong to us—to the church—we do bear a share of responsibility for the havoc they create when they get loose in our neighborhoods.*

So what are we to do? In my title, I refer to 'Breath' to evoke the image of God as Spirit, Wind, Breath. And the question before us then is this: when we get clobbered again and again by these texts that can seem so full of hatred for who we are—these texts that lead Pastor Fred Phelps to proclaim "God hates fags"—how in the face of such hate do we keep from having the Breath of God knocked right out of us? That's the initial challenge.

One way to meet this challenge is to set these texts within their literary, theological and historical context: to understand these verses within their original languages, within the chapters and books where they appear, within the theological perspective of their authors, and within the historical eras that they originated. And this helps quite a bit, because it is very difficult upon close examination to maintain that the Bible explicitly condemns the caring and committed same-sex relationships that seek recognition and affirmation in the church today. So, while we must do better than this, we can at least begin here.

Leviticus 18:22 and 20:13 both clearly voice a prohibition against same-sex activity between men. Both verses forbid a man "to lie with a man as with a woman." They call it an "abomination," a translation of a Hebrew word which is rather ambiguous in its precise meaning, but which certainly does not suggest approval.

But there are very good reasons to doubt that this prohibition had anything like loving, monogamous same-sex relationships in mind. First, we know historically that there was same-sex activity between men that the early Hebrews would have known about and might have wanted to prohibit. It fell into two categories. One was ritual sex enacted between male priests at pagan temples as part of various fertility rituals. This form of sexual activity was undoubtedly seen as a form of idolatrous worship, and Israel had a bad habit of trying out the worship practices of its neighbors, so this prohibition may reflect that concern. The other form was a sort of military "hazing" where victorious male soldiers raped the members of the beaten army in a display of dominance and humiliation. This form of same-sex activity is well known still today both in prisons and in war. It has nothing to do with human love, and it would rightly be offensive to Israel's sense of human dignity. So there are solid historical reasons to say that these verses, neither in the past nor in the present, have the purpose of condemning consensual, personal, gay relationships.

There are also literary reasons to set them aside. Both passages are contained in that part of Leviticus called the "Holiness Code," a series of strict commands and prohibitions designed to maintain Israel's distinct identity among its neighbors. The root word for "holiness" here simply means "kept separate," and the prohibitions of the Holiness Code were determined to define Israel in contrast to its neighbors. In short, if they're doing it, then we can't. In this sense the "holiness" of the code is really more about ethnic purity then about human morality. The holiness code prohibits sowing two types of seed in the same field, crossbreeding two types of cattle, storing different types of food in the same cupboard, blending different types of thread in the same cloth, and so forth. It is a way of drawing clear boundaries between peoples based on how we choose to arrange the world and how others do. So these verses are intended to meticulously craft and preserve the ethnic-religious identity of a people 3000 years ago. Whatever their wisdom then, it does not speak easily to us today. Virtually nothing in the Holiness Code commands our attention any longer—and for good reason.

The other commonly invoked Old Testament passage is the story of the destruction of the cities of Sodom and Gomorrah, recounted in Genesis 19. This text quite clearly portrays the threat of gang rape—not consensual sex—yet it still managed to give us our English word "sodomy," thereby making the mere description of same-sex activity an implicit judgment of it at the same time.

There is much that could be said about this text, but it is enough to mention several things. Sodom and Gomorrah were marked for divine destruction *prior to* the incident at Lot's doorstep. Whatever they were condemned for happened *before* the angelic messengers arrived in town. In fact, when Sodom and Gomorrah are mentioned elsewhere in the Bible (except for one obscure reference in the book of Jude) they are universally acknowledged, by both the prophets (e.g., Isaiah 1:10-17; 3:9-15; Ezekiel 16:49) and Jesus (Matthew 11:19,24; Luke 10:12), as examples of communities where injustice toward the vulnerable ran rampant. In short, they were known for their obscene inhospitality—of which their behavior toward the angelic messengers is simply one more bit of damning evidence.

It is hard for us to imagine the esteem for hospitality in the ancient world, but it ran high enough that Lot was willing to offer his own daughters to the crowd—clearly in his mind they were hungry for sexual violence, not homosexual activity. It may also be hard for us to imagine that this text says more about hospitality than homosexuality because *if that's true*—and I think clearly it is—*then "sodomy" as a derogatory term really names the church's sin of inhospitality toward homosexuals rather than naming the activity that occurs between homosexuals.* This text, too, does *not* have our gay brothers (or our lesbian sisters) in mind.

Turning to the New Testament, I Corinthians 6:9 and I Timothy 1:10 both employ obscure Greek words that have sometimes been translated in ways that appear to condemn homosexuality. The words (*arsenokoita* and *malakoi*), which literally mean "men who penetrate" and "men who are soft," may refer to partners in a homosexual act, though we cannot say for certain. But if they do, then historically they most likely have in mind the practice, once common among Greco-Roman men but falling into disrepute by Paul's time, of pederasty. This involved a heterosexual man taking a prepubescent boy as a tool for sexual pleasure. Such relationships were entirely about the gratification of the man and the domination of the boy; like hazing, they sought to inscribe into the boy's character and into his body the power structures of a very hierarchical and patriarchal society. Given Paul's vision of life in Christ where all are members of one body without power distinctions, it would be no surprise if Paul found pederasty a particularly distasteful and anti-Gospel behavior.

Because the words in question here are used nowhere else in either the New Testament or in other Greek writings of the era, we can only guess at what they meant for Paul. But to guess that they condemn the committed relationships of gay and lesbian Christians undoubtedly reflects the prejudices of the church today rather than the mind of Paul 2000 years ago.

Finally, Romans 1:26-27 is the most controversial of these passages. It reads, "For this reason [that is, on account of their idolatry] God gave them [that is, the Gentiles] up to degrading passions. Their women exchanged natural intercourse for unnatural, and in the same way also the men, giving up natural intercourse with women, were consumed with passion for one another."

There are conservative scholars who are willing to admit that none of the other passages constitute a judgment against contemporary expressions of homosexuality, but who still find in this text everything they need to support their view. This passage is tugged at from many angles, pulled in many different directions, and by its many different interpreters. It is a textbook case of utter ambiguity. Much of this has to do with how one understands Paul's use of "natural" and "unnatural" here, which is far from clear. He certainly does not use the word "unnatural" to show his admiration for same-sex activity, but the word used is not a word of clear condemnation either. It may suggest moral judgment or it may imply a charge of being culturally backward but not sinful. Both readings can be supported. And later on, in Romans 11:24, Paul uses the same word—"unnatural"—to describe God's actions in bringing the Gentiles into the church. There it simply means the utterly surprising, who-would-have-guessed character of God's activity. In any case, it is hardly wise to let so much hate hinge on the interpretation of a single word that is fiercely contested by scholars on both sides.

Rather than try to discuss in detail the many divergent interpretations of this text, we might see that this much *is* clear and acknowledged by everyone: Paul's purpose in Romans 1 is to declare the utter sinfulness of the Gentiles. But his purpose in Romans 2 is to make painfully clear the equally utter sinfulness of the Jews. Chapter 2 begins, "Therefore you have no excuse, whoever you are, when you judge another; for in passing judgment on anyone else you condemn yourself, because you, the judge, are doing the very same things." Paul is not concerned with the details; *he is concerned to indict the entire human race without exception* . . . and then, in Romans 3, he introduces the grace of God—*for absolutely everyone.* Regardless of Paul's historical position on "homosexuality" (which remains far from certain), if he were to hear Romans 1 quoted by one group of persons to condemn another group of persons *he would explode in anger.* To use the passage this way flies in the face of the very argument Paul is making, which is to silence judgment and announce grace.

So, to conclude this first half of my presentation, I think we can say with great confidence that the Bible contains not a single passage that can be said to clearly condemn caring, committed, Christian homosexual relationships. The biblical authors simply never imagined and never addressed this issue.

***

But. Yes, there is a "but." But even seeing that all of these texts can be disarmed, they *still* dominate the conversation in the church in an irrational and—if we are honest—in a hateful way. We still find ourselves again and again needing to protect ourselves, less from the texts themselves than from the fear and judgment and hate they seem quite able to perpetuate, regardless of our scholarly insight. How do we explain that? And how do we *change* that?

I believe it happens because the root of sin—the very essence of the human fall—is the temptation to break relationship. And while its extreme form occurs in acts like murder and rape, its more subtle and far more common form is to use morality to break relationship. The narrative of the fall in the Garden of Eden is profoundly true in saying that the root of sin lies in our desire—against God's better judgment—to claim for ourselves the knowledge of good and evil. Because this knowledge consistently sows the seeds of self-righteousness (or self-loathing) in ourselves, and just as consistently sows the seeds of judgment and exclusion in our attitudes toward others.

God can know the goodness and the evil of our actions and yet love us undeterred by this knowledge. But we, we are entangled—addicted is not too strong a word—in a pattern of using this stolen knowledge to draw lines to define who's 'in' and who's 'out,' who's 'us' and who's 'them,' who's 'worthy'—and who's not. And these six texts play to that impulse all too well. They sit like the tree at the center of the Garden, ever tempting us to eat of their fruit and become like gods. Which is why explaining these texts is not enough. Explanations may afford us a measure of protection from the terror they have often inflicted on us, but explanations are not likely to move the church to offer us the welcome for which we wait.

Indeed, some will respond that our explanations only show that we are looking to explain away those passages that trouble us. That we are not interested in taking the Bible seriously. *And we need to counter that charge aggressively and articulately. Because it is precisely a rigidly literal reading of the Bible that fails to take Scripture seriously enough.* And out of faithfulness to God, we must be willing to say that.

We desperately need to refashion the way that we, as a whole church, tend to relate to Scripture. In our own rush to explain these passages there lies an implicit fear that if we could not explain them we would need to condemn ourselves—even if that self-condemnation flew in the face of our lived existence, our loved relationships with each other and our own interior sense of God's affirmation. Such willingness—often implied even on *our* part—to

101

bind the whole of God's mystery to the fixed text of the Bible distorts the very purpose of Scripture.

The biblical text is not sacred because it has captured and frozen the whole of God within its pages. Indeed, this is precisely why God distrusts Israel's desire to build a Temple: lest a fixed structure imply that God is anything less than the Absolute Freedom to Liberate and to Gather that is revealed in the name "I will be who I will be." Rather, the text is sacred because it has the capacity to bring us into a relationship with the Living God, the God who is no less capable of surprising us today than of surprising Israel and the early church in the past. Our primary relationship as Christians is not to the written text, but to the Living God. And whenever we forget this, we are no longer regarding the book as sacred but are beginning to revere it as an idol.

Let me say that more pointedly. The sacredness of this text is *not* that it is untouched, unmarred, by the human limitations—the time-bound knowledge and attitudes—of its authors. *It is*. No less than the stories it contains, the text as a whole bears powerful witness to a God who is willing and determined to take the risk of working within the limits and imperfections (as well as within the best aspirations) of human beings. The Bible is filled with such stories. The sacredness of the text is that, in the midst of these human limits, imperfections, and aspirations, it continues to invite us into real relationship with the God who promises, even today, to be doing a new thing (Is. 43:19).

So rather than just intellectually explaining away the condemnation that these texts have often borne for us, *we must show that we read them as we do out of a deep relationship with the Living God to whom the Bible does bear witness but who the mystery of whom the Bible does not exhaust.* One evocative way we can articulate this is to be clear to others that *we read the Bible faithfully—"Word by Word" while "holding our Breath."*

By the image of "holding our Breath" I mean to say that we read these texts—and all biblical texts—holding in us the loving, creative, and life-giving Breath of God that moved over the face of the deep at the dawn of creation. We read them holding the Breath of God that promised faithfulness to Abraham and Sara—if only they would join in a journey to a land they'd never seen. And the Breath of God that spoke to Moses from a burning bush and promised liberation to a people in bondage.

We read them holding the Breath of God that filled the prophets' words like Holy Wind: moving Hosea (2:23) to tell those called "Not my People" that they were indeed "My People." Moving Jeremiah (7:4) to warn those chanting, "This is the Temple of the Lord," that no such chanting could limit the Freedom of God. Moving Amos (5:24) to proclaim that the *only* worship that truly honors God is worship filled—like rushing water—with justice and mercy. And moving Isaiah to explode in anger against those who failed to welcome home their own kin . . . and then to boldly declare that God was gathering in these outcasts—and to promise that there were yet more outcasts to gather in (Is. 56, 58). This gathering Breath even inspires the author of Jonah to tell an imaginative tale in which not simply outcasts but Israel's *outright enemies* are gathered into God's care.

Throughout Israel's story of God, this Holy Breath is active stretching the people's imagination about what God can do and about whom God can include in this unfolding story. And because this is the Breath that we hold in our lungs—and in our hearts—as we read the Bible we may lament those texts that fail to billow with this Holy Wind, but they cannot frighten us. *We take Scripture far too seriously for that.* For the very Breath that surprised Israel by blowing into unexpected places has blown into our own lives as well. And who are we—who is anyone—to say that God's Breath cannot do that?

By the image of "reading the Bible Word by Word" I am suggesting that any serious and faithful reading of the Bible involves setting every *written* word within the context of the *lived* Word of Jesus the Christ. In his life we see the Breath of God take on full flesh. He spoke always of the Kingdom of God, a phrase that in his day turned the very notion of kingship inside out. Today we might better capture the sense of it by hearing him declare the Kin-dom of God, the divine activity through which God makes all of us kin. In his ministry—from the subversive stories he told, to the bodies he healed and restored to community, to the outcast company he kept, to the festive and inclusive meals he shared—we see an astonishing revelation, a scandalous *enactment* of God's gathering love. It is a love that gathers even when that gathering angers the religious leaders whose imaginations have grown too brittle to be stretched by God. And it is a gathering love that suffers death without ever betraying or denying those who have been gathered in.

So we read these texts, these words so often wielded as weapons against us, we read them alongside this Living Word who simply says, "Come. Sit with me. Share my table. For I have called you by name, and you are mine." And when we find ourselves in the company of this One from Nazareth, it is not the intellectual explanations that drain the power from these texts, it is the sheer joy of his presence, and the company of his friends who welcome us. Reading the Bible "word by Word" reminds us that some words are no more than old wineskins, destined to be burst by New Wine.

So we must counter these texts not simply by dismissing them with scholarship—though there is much that we can dismiss in that way. But to really heal the wounds in ourselves—and in our accusers—we must bear bold witness to the overarching Breath of God's gathering grace and to the Gospel of the same gathering grace made known in Jesus Christ. We can do this by holding our Breath while we read the Bible word by Word.

***

Finally, if we are blunt, I am here tonight, and you are here tonight, not simply because we are wrestling with the sacredness of this text, but because we are wrestling with the sacredness of our sex. Were it not for that, the text would never become a problem in the first place. So let me close with a few thoughts about the sex that sits at the center of this.

Earlier I suggested that the root of human sinfulness is our addiction to making judgments about good and evil in ways that become judgments about who is worthy of love and life, who is welcome in the "household of us"—which often gets misrepresented as the "household of God." We do this in many ways, but sexuality has a uniquely powerful place in this dynamic of sin, making it a favorite reference point for conveying or denying worthiness. *Now let me be very clear:* this is *not* because sex is intrinsically sinful as we have sometimes (often!) been taught. *It is because sex is potentially sacred—and is therefore a target for distortion by forces opposed to God.*

While sin is intrinsically about the breaking of relationships, sexuality is our embodied drive to unite with other persons. It is that deep longing to be naked not just in our skin but also in our soul, and to be thus in the presence of another, and to feel ourselves unconditionally welcomed and named worthy by them. Sexuality, in its best expression, is a tactile echo of the tender intimacy with which God knows each of us. And because of that capacity to be a human ground of grace, it becomes a place where sin tempts us to most vigorously divide ourselves and to deny grace to others.

We sense intuitively—but without fully realizing what's at stake—that what transpires in our sexual encounters is (or can be) something of profound importance. It can also, of course, and for the same reasons, be of devastating consequence or have a cheapening effect. So it is not surprising that sexuality is one of the landscapes on which morality gets turned away from questions of ethical integrity and pressed into the unholy work of measuring human worth.

But I want to leave you with this set of questions, because we really can't stop here. What might it mean if our sexuality, like the best passages in the Bible, billowed full with the Breath of God? What might it mean to claim our sexuality as a fine place for the Word to become flesh yet again? Playfully put, yet seriously posed, what might it mean to speak of "sex—in the city—of God"?

That's a whole other talk, but it is *the essential question to ask* as we move beyond these texts themselves. If Scripture does not condemn our sexuality, then what might it offer for positive guidance to shape our sexuality? In treating the texts tonight, I suggested that the Breath of God manifest in Israel's life and the Word of God manifest in Jesus' life have been characterized most clearly by acts of care and nurture, welcome and worth-giving, justice and mercy. When the joyful abandon of our sexual relationships, both within the bedroom and within our common life, is also marked as by these things—care and nurture, welcome and worth-giving, justice and mercy—well, that is what sex in the city of God looks like. You see, when our sexual lives display these same features—features which are not tied to the gender of our partner but to the quality of our relationship—then we can rejoice knowing that in our bodies we indeed hold the Breath of God and that in our flesh the Word again becomes Incarnate Love.

This essay comments on a rather parochial event, the censure and admonishment of a Minneapolis church, but the dynamics at play are present in many other places and denominations. An abridged version of this essay ran in the November issue of the Metro Lutheran; the full version appeared in the December issue of the Lutherans Concerned/Twin Cities newsletter.

23. Friends in High Places
(November 2004)

I want to comment here—with uncomfortable candor—on Bishop Craig Johnson's letter of censure and admonition to Bethany Lutheran Church. "Uncomfortable" because I count Bishop Johnson as a public friend, both to the Reconciling in Christ program and to the place of GLBT persons in the church. "With candor" because as we approach the 2005 Churchwide Assembly, how the struggle of GLBT people for full recognition within the church gets framed in the wider church matters a great deal. And, in his letter of censure and admonition, Bishop Johnson has framed Bethany's piece of this struggle in a manner that is neither very fair to Bethany nor very helpful to the wider church.

In September, Bishop Johnson censured and admonished Bethany Lutheran Church for the call and ordination of Jay Wiesner. While Jay is a seminary graduate and fully trained for ministry, his decision to be in a committed same-sex relationship makes him ineligible for placement on the ELCA clergy roster. So Bethany did exactly what the bishop censured and admonished them for: they called into ordained ministry someone ineligible for such call under current ELCA guidelines. And a formal letter of rebuke was really the lightest of the disciplinary options open to the bishop. (He chose to postpone any further discipline until after the 2005 Churchwide Assembly, allowing Bethany's ministry, both at the parish/neighborhood level and also at the Synod level, where Jay sits on the Synod Council, to go on unhindered for the moment.)

But the bishop missed an important opportunity to show something far more significant than forbearance. He had an opportunity to speak forthrightly about the stakes involved here for the whole people of God—to be at once pastoral and prophetic—but his letter is neither. Instead it engages in "churchspeak," language about what it means to be the church—as an institution—with barely a reference to the actual flesh and blood people of God who comprise the church (or are marginalized by the church).

Bishop Johnson speaks of Bethany breaking their "covenant" with the ELCA over call procedures, but mentions nothing of the covenant with the gospel of Jesus Christ to which Bethany felt a greater loyalty. He speaks of Bethany's decision to "pre-empt" the current ELCA study process, putting ordained leaders, both locally and nationally, "in a difficult position." He laments the "strain" their action places on their relationship with the Oromo Lutheran Church (with whom they share their building). But he is silent—utterly silent—on the excruciating position, the sometimes suicidal strain, that years of church study alongside ongoing policies of implicit judgment have placed tens of thousands of gay and lesbian Lutherans in. Jeremiah might well accuse him of claiming "peace, peace," when there is no peace, as though fidelity to an institutional covenant that exacts untold suffering from "the least of these" is the sort of peace that Christ brings.

Most egregiously in my mind, while framing his own decision as one made "after much prayer and listening," he says simply that Bethany acted "after debate, discussion, and vote." Yes, they did. But I attended the September Synod Council meeting at which Bishop Johnson sought input from his Council and invited testimony from members of Bethany before making his decision about disciplinary action; and if you ask anyone in the room that day, he or she will tell you to a person, that *more than anything else Bethany Lutheran Church acted after prayer.* Person after person from Bethany described the prayerful process. So much so that several members of the Council, including some who disagreed with Bethany's action, commended them for the evident way that their act of ecclesial disobedience was grounded in prayer. *By erasing this prayerful component of their action from view by the whole church, the bishop's letter reduces it to a matter of rebellious impatience when it was clearly perceived as and presented by Bethany as an act of prayerful obedience to the Spirit.*

It was telling that no one from Bethany pleaded for leniency from the Council or the bishop. They fully expected to experience consequences for their action, and no one sought to avoid them. In fact, when one member of the Council asked, rather reprovingly, whether they had weighed the possible consequences of going forward with the ordination, one Bethany member replied quite soberly, "Yes, but in all honesty we were more concerned about the possible consequences if we chose not to go forward." Right or wrong, Bethany's point of reference was not church polity but their deep yearning to respond faithfully to the gospel—and they saw these two aspirations set in conflict here. But Bishop Johnson's letter nowhere acknowledges this, adopting instead the tone of a paternalistic parent chastising an unruly child.

I do not mean to suggest that Bishop Johnson ought simply to have looked the other way. He is surely right, as he says, to be "mindful of my responsibility and promise to uphold the constitution of our church," but he is equally responsible to be truthful to the wider church in how he portrays those who fall under his discipline. He clearly *could* have censured and admonished Bethany for their transgression of ELCA polity while *also* expressly noting that their prayerful action now becomes part of the ELCA's ongoing process of discernment. In fact, *I think he owed them at least that much.* He also could have acknowledged that time may yet show that Bethany's actions did indeed reflect the Spirit's leading, even while finding himself compelled to censure them in the mean time.

Obviously, as well, Bethany simply could have waited another year (as the bishop requested) to see what the 2005 Churchwide Assembly brought. But that option is 'obvious' only if you forget the impatient eagerness of the Ethiopian eunuch in Acts 8, or the immediacy of Peter's decision to baptize Gentiles in Act 10, or Jesus' readiness to heal on the Sabbath rather than wait just a few hours to avoid scandal. Such passages hardly prove the wisdom of Bethany's decision, but they do require us to measure that decision with the memory of the Spirit's freedom close at hand. Unfortunately, the bishop's letter forgets to remember—or to remind the church—that the Spirit blows where it will . . . sometimes from the very center, sometimes from the edges.

We may well need the bishop's friendship in the days ahead, but I will say this with uncomfortable candor: *what we need from the bishop is friendship that does not erase either our prayers or our pain from the wider church.* And more than this, what we need *from ourselves* is the determination and creativity to insure that the church hears us and sees us with or without the help of our friends.

108

I penned this essay in the first two hours after the release of the ELCA Sexuality Task Force's Report and Recommendations in January 2005. At the time I was at Faith Lutheran Church in Houston, Texas, preparing to begin a weekend training for the Reconciling in Christ program. There was something both disorienting and gracious about receiving word of these recommendations so far from home and yet in such good company. It eventually appeared in the March issue of the Lutherans Concerned/Twin Cities newsletter.

24. "Those Papers Belong to Me"
(January 13, 2005)

Ten of us gathered at the front of the sanctuary for evening vespers. It happened to be the eve of the release of the ELCA Sexuality Task Force recommendations on blessings and ordination of gays and lesbians, but that was just a coincidence. We would have been here anyway. We gathered, as folks do every Wednesday evening at this Lutheran church, and prayed, not just for ourselves, but for our church and for the whole people of God.

And we woke the next morning to find that more than half of us had been, yet again, politely erased from the Body of Christ. At some point oppression, even when framed in gentle gracious words, deserves outrage in response.

This is what they recommend that our church do with us: Having listened to our brothers and sisters, having scoured our tradition, and having studied the Scripture, they can find no compelling reason—neither within a theology of grace nor within a Gospel that calls us unequivocally to love one another—to endorse a ceremony that would bless our love and extend to our lives the prayerful support and celebration of the church. Yes, they will allow for individual pastors and congregations to do this as an expression of pastoral care, but our church as a whole will not conspire with (that is, will not "breathe with") God to bless the love that blesses us.

And again, having listened, scoured, and studied, they can find no compelling reason—neither within the repeatedly unexpected gathering activity of God in the Old Testament nor within radically inclusive ministry of Jesus or the widening movement of the Spirit in the New Testament—to dare to lead the rest of the church to consider that God is doing a new thing even now by calling some of us into ordained ministry while also blessing our lives with committed relationships. Again, they will allow individual congregations, with the approval of their respective bishops and synods, to call and ordain us without fear of discipline, but our church as a whole will not say "yes," to the call that God has placed in our hearts.

Some will say we should celebrate these as small victories. But I say, NO. *We do not live with—we are not loved by—a God who trades in small victories. Ours is a God who frees the captives rather than negotiating more lenient terms of captivity.* Moses said simply to Pharaoh, "Thus says the Lord, Let my people go." Isaiah said simply to Israel, "What do you mean by crushing my people, by grinding the face of the poor?" When will our church hear these words?

Paul, likening the diversity of the early church to a human body wrote sternly to the church at Corinth lest any "eye say to the hand, 'I have no need of you'." Peter, seeing the movement of the Spirit in lives he never expected said simply, "How dare we withhold from those who have received from the Spirit?" And Jesus said, in words intended as encouragement, but which have today become words of judgment on this church, "Whatever you do to the least of these, my brothers and sisters, you do to me." When will our church hear these words?

And so, we are again marginalized, reminded that we are, of course, welcome—so long as we take our place at the back of the bus, in the shadows of the sanctuary, and so long as we are quiet and well-behaved.

Undeniably this church is deeply divided over whether we belong here and on what terms. There are good people "bound by conscience" on both sides of the question. Yet Jesus knew, as well, that there were good people both for and against healing on the Sabbath, both for and against touching lepers, both for and against chatting with Samaritans, both for and against blessing children, both for and against feasting with outcasts. He didn't try to find a pastoral middle. He found the outer edge and said—loudly—that God was there. I imagine that's why he got killed. Apparently it isn't something the church cares to imitate anymore today.

I will be watching closely this August, when the ELCA votes on the Task Force recommendations. Because I know this, that if our church indeed votes to formally offer us "full" second-class citizenship papers in the Kingdom of God, Jesus will be first in line to say, "those papers belong to me."

This letter, written in the aftermath of the Report and Recommendations by the ELCA Sexuality Task Force and dated on January 18, the Confession of St. Peter, seeks to recall to the church's leadership the role that it can play it issues like this—not to take sides but to convene stories.

25. An Open Letter to the ELCA Bishops and Synod Vice-Presidents
(January 18, 2005)

Dear brothers and sisters in Christ,

Many persons will hope to bend your ears in the weeks ahead regarding the recommendations of the Sexuality Task Force. I am but one of them, so I will be brief. I am sending this letter to every bishop and every Synod Council vice-president.

I am a lay theologian, with graduate degrees in both Theology and Christian Ethics. I have taught at two Lutheran colleges and have worked closely as an ally with both GLBT youth and adults. I presently direct the Reconciling in Christ Program in the Twin Cities area. Foremost, however, I am a baptized child of God driven to speak with deep conviction in this moment. I pray that you will at least read this letter.

The issue of full participation of gay and lesbian persons in the church does not rest finally on Scriptural arguments any more than did the issue of full participation for Gentiles in the early church. There—as here—the issue rests on whether the outpouring of the Spirit can be discerned in the lives of persons that neither the early church nor the present church could have anticipated.

That this story (from Acts 10) was not included in the *Journey Together Faithfully* study materials insured that the biblical evidence would be weighed in such a manner as to hinder the movement of the Spirit in the study process. This was not a minor oversight or an unfortunate omission—it was a lapse that undercut the very integrity of the study process because it kept off the table the biblical mandate that we *must* attend carefully and openly to the possible movement of the Spirit in the lives of the people whose fate we are discussing.

This is where you now have a deep responsibility. In Acts 10 the believers from Joppa have an encounter with Cornelius and the rest of his Gentile household. That encounter not only alters their lives but reshapes the life of the early church—and does so in an "unbiblical" way—that is, in a way not bounded by Scripture, attesting to the freedom of God to indeed "gather others besides those already gathered." (Is. 56:8) These believers have this encounter for one reason only—*because they followed Peter to Cornelius' house.*

In the church today, *you are Peter.* As bishops and synod presidents you are responsible for seeing that the believers from Joppa close their Bibles long enough to discern whether the Spirit has indeed been unexpectedly poured out upon the household of Cornelius today. Between now and August you have but one clear mandate in this regard, and that is to ensure that this meeting happens. In every conference of every synod you must see to it that listening events are held at which every voting delegate to the Churchwide Assembly truly meets the household of Cornelius. This is *not* a call for a "fair and balanced" presentation of both sides. *It is a call that you provide simply—and essentially—a moment in which one thing alone happens: the believers from Joppa listen to the stories of faith told by the household of Cornelius.* Nothing more. Nothing less.

If we as a church fail to make certain that this meeting happens in full earnestness and with genuine openness, then we have failed to be a people who take seriously the meaning of Pentecost.

With deepest prayers for your leadership in the days ahead,
David Weiss

This is my most complete response to the ELCA Task Force Report and Recommendations. It evolved over several weeks, beginning in late January with the claim that we need to close our Bibles for a few months. That original essay appeared in the March issue of the Lutherans Concerned/Twin Cities newsletter, with an abridged versions appearing in the Metro Lutheran and on the website for Lutheran magazine. When the Concord, the quarterly newsletter for Lutherans Concerned/North America asked me to address the Report and Recommendations directly, I developed this longer version, which appeared in the March Concord.

26. It's Time to Close our Bibles for a Few Months
(January/February 2005)

The January release of the Sexuality Task Force recommendations confirmed what many of us feared: the ELCA still does not really want—or yet know how—to address the place of gay and lesbian persons in the church. There were those on the Task Force, gay, lesbian, and ally, who pressed for more than what the final report offered. I respect their work and I share their anguish at a report—and an entire process—that fell so far short of its potential. But I will not try to look on the bright side of recommendations that would, in effect, establish Jim Crow laws for the church.

The Task Force makes three recommendations (you can find the complete report at: www.elca.org/faithfuljourney). The first encourages the church to "concentrate on finding ways to live together faithfully in the midst of our disagreements." Amen. But the study process itself, despite an investment of several years and more than $1 million, failed to do this in some pretty significant ways, so these words lack credibility in my mind.

The second recommendation urges the ELCA to "continue to respect the pastoral guidance of the 1993 statement of the Conference of Bishops" regarding the blessing of same sex couples. But in 1993 the bishops explicitly refused to approve of any such blessing ceremony, promising only "to express trust in and continue dialogue with those pastors and congregations who are in ministry with gay and lesbian persons"—as though gay and lesbian persons exist only in those congregations who knowingly and willingly minister to them. And the Task Force comments that blessing ceremonies ought not imply approval of these relationships and that they should "be understood as a matter quite distinct from and in no way equivalent to marriage." This is a "pastoral guidance" with a pretty sour aftertaste. It not only fails to carry us forward at all, it goes out of its way to ensure that no one imagines we are moving at all.

The third recommendation, concerning the ordination of persons in committed same-sex relationships, is simply abusive in extolling the capricious use of ecclesial power. It recommends, almost unbelievably, that the ELCA continue its policy of excluding partnered gay or lesbian persons from ordained ministry, but suggests that it "*may refrain*" from enforcing this policy. This is *not* a glimmer of hope; *it is a recommendation to informally institutionalize the very divisions that the task force laments.* It is a recommendation that we become a church of red synods and blue synods, red bishops and blue bishops. More pointedly, *that we become a church in which some synods own slaves while others do not.* And now, whether any one of us is "slave" or "free" at any particular moment depends not on the claim of God on our life but on the temperament of the bishop, the synod council, and/or the candidacy committee.

Yes, as everyone keeps reminding me, the Task Force's recommendations are just that: a series of recommendations, a beginning place, with lots of opportunity for input from Bishops, Councils, Divisions, and Synod Assemblies along the way to Churchwide in August. But it's a *lousy beginning place*. Moreover, while legislative strategizing—drafting and shepherding resolutions—is undeniably important, this is, finally, not about a vote; it is about a struggle for the heart and the soul of our church.

So I suggest that whatever resolutions we put forward, this ought to be foremost among them: *that as a church it's time for us to close our Bibles for a few months.* We won't find the answer we're looking for there—at least not in the places we've been led to look.

We haven't even asked the right question yet. We've supposedly been studying whether to offer blessings to same-sex couples and whether to ordain persons in committed relationships. Yet in reality the study materials led us to and mired us in a quite different question: whether homosexuality, either in orientation or expression (and it's just plain arrogant when straight people assume a distinction between the two) is sinful. But this has never been the right question. The church has only ever blessed heterosexual marriages *between sinners*. The church has only ever ordained pastors *who have also been sinners*. And don't let anyone say that "willful, ongoing" sin is the crucial distinction. We regularly bless marriages between persons quite willfully devoted to conspicuous consumption. We don't hesitate to ordain people who smoke. The "sin" question misses the point.

Even the questions about blessing and ordination are misguided. They're so specific that they've kept us from seeing the question that would offer us a way forward: *How should the church respond when persons come seeking full participation as they are, without becoming like the majority?* Especially when they are persons who the Bible has seemed to suggest have no part among God's people unless they change their ways? *That's the situation we face.* And that's the situation faced by the early church when the Gentiles sought full participation without the precondition of first becoming Jewish in diet and circumcision.

Acts 10, 11, and 15 tell us how the early church responded to that situation, but the Task Force specifically chose *not* to include those texts in the *Journey Together Faithfully* study materials. They *set aside* the one biblical model for constructively engaging our situation. No wonder we got nowhere.

In contrast, the early church did not rush back to the Torah to see whether Gentiles needed to be circumcised in order to join the church. If they had, they would've gotten mired in the same dilemma we are, asking whether what the Torah seemed to say about Gentiles 'back then' still applied in the first century. And while there were some who wanted to do that, the church dared to try a different approach, deciding *to listen to the lives* of the Gentiles who sought to join them.

Rather than quoting biblical texts or insisting on always having "fair and balanced" opposing views, the early church simply and attentively listened to the stories of God's activity in their lives. Then the church asked, is it possible that God's Spirit is already active in the lives of these people in ways we would never have guessed? Is it possible that God is surprising us even now? *These are the questions that our church must ask today.* And these questions will only be asked if we all close our Bibles long enough so that at least the voting delegates to Churchwide are compelled to quietly and respectfully listen to the lives of those gay and lesbian Christians who stand before the church today. That's the resolution that will make all the other resolutions worthwhile.

Because were the church actually to do that, I suspect that many—a majority, *a two-thirds majority even*—would find themselves saying, "I'm not sure exactly how to square up the biblical passages, but after truly listening to the stories of these people I have to agree with Peter (Acts 10:47), 'How can we as a church withhold blessings and ordinations from these persons whom God has so clearly blessed with love and/or called to ministry?'"

There is time before August to create sufficiently safe moments in which our stories can be heard, in which this church can truly ask whether there is evidence of the Spirit active in our lives. But we'll all need to close our Bibles for a few months if that's to happen. And according to Acts that might even be the most biblical thing we could do.

This short parable, loosely echoing Jesus' tale of the Samaritan (Luke 10:25-37), comments on the same-sex marriage issue raging in Minnesota during the spring of 2005.

27. Who is my Neighbor?
(April 2005)

And in answer to this question the Teacher said:

"A small band of people set out from Jericho for Jerusalem. There were men walking with men and women walking with women. There was joy on their faces. And you could hear it, too, in the laughter of the children that darted among them. They were going to Jerusalem in order to celebrate the love that they had found in each other. They walked with eagerness, but also with anxiety, for they knew this journey was not without risk. But then, how can love be content to remain hidden? How can love not long to be known and celebrated in a wider community? And so, despite the risks, they went.

"Now before long other persons on the road noticed their hand-holding and their joy and these persons found themselves uncomfortable. These were good persons, devoutly religious. They were many in number and came from all walks of life, including pastors and elected officials. And they did not wish to see this band of people reach Jerusalem. So they passed laws and proposed amendments; they held rallies and set up websites. And their message was: in this land only those whose love is exactly like ours may go to Jerusalem. For others there shall be no recognition, no rights. Their love is to be hidden from view; they are not part of us. And these people did all that they could to slow down the small band. But still, they walked forward.

"But along this same road, certain other people began to jeer the small band, calling out names like faggot and dyke, and words like pervert and queer. Emboldened by these words, other persons picked up rocks and started throwing them, so that the small band huddled close together on the road. Finally, still others moved forward with clubs and bats and began to swing at the people, beating them to the edge of death while the children scattered screaming into the desert. And then the crowd dispersed, leaving them to die.

"But this was a well-traveled road, and before long others came upon the scene. They saw that some of the bodies were badly hurt while others had wounded spirits. They saw the children trembling in fear in the distance. Now these were also good persons, strong in their faith. Their numbers, too, included pastors and even elected officials. But though they murmured soft words of sympathy, they did nothing more. They were afraid of what it might cost them to offer aid these persons. So they passed by on the other side of the road and lamented to themselves that the world was such a dangerous place to be.

"And finally, as the sun was setting, another group of persons came along. They were fewer in number, but still there was a remarkable diversity among them. Here, too, there were at least a few pastors and elected officials. And while some of these persons considered themselves religious, others did not. In fact, some of these persons even disdained the church. And yet, when this group of persons came upon this small band, now beaten and scattered, this is what they did. They tended the wounds. They gathered the children. They comforted the despairing. And they took the small band to an inn at the outskirts of Jerusalem, where they made arrangements for them to stay. And they said to the innkeeper, 'Tonight we are going away to organize. We will be back tomorrow to settle the bill—and to build a society in which all love is honored, in which all children are prized, in which all families are safe, and in which understanding and respect guide our common life.'"

And the Teacher turned to the crowd, many of whom were shifting uneasily from one foot to the foot, and he said, "Who among these acted as neighbor toward those in need? Go and do likewise."

Good poetry has a guerrilla dimension to it, subverting the familiar and inviting us to see connections we didn't expect—and perhaps didn't want to see. Unlike more direct forms of communication, it speaks to us while "our guard is down," which is precisely why the powerful mistrust the poets. To a poet, "the way things are" is never more than provisional, never beyond imaginative challenge, never immune to the lure of a different vision. Such poetry has the capacity to be prophetic in its truest sense. Here, "with Orlando on my mind," I offer seven short poems that try to speak the truth of our hopes and convictions. They are a bit awkward in form, in part because this journey to Churchwide 2005 has been undeniably awkward, but also because the acrostic form itself becomes part of the guerrilla art, speaking—as we do ourselves—from the margin. (Acrostic poems use the first letter of each line, read down along the left margin, to spell out an extra message.)

28. A Set of Seven . . . With Orlando on my Mind: Acrostics with a Prophetic Edge
(April 2005)

Are we wet yet?

Let those with ears hear:
each child brought to the font
takes on Christ.

Jew or Greek, slave or free, male or female,
under this water
such words lose their power
to divide us or to lure us
into yet another fall, as though
christian identity were not
entirely wrought by water and Word.

Raised up, too, with Christ,
our brothers and sisters,
lesbian and gay, are marked, not by their
love, but by the same cross that marks us.

Dare we deny the water
or the Word that
welcomed them then—and
now—into the Body of Christ?

(Amos 5:24, Galatians 3:27-28)

Brimstone aimed our way

Sodom and Gomorrah will get
off easier by far,
despite their horrific inhospitality, than
other communities who fail to welcome
messengers sent two by two (still today) by Jesus;
yet we repeat Sodom's sin and blame it on those sent.

(Luke 10:10-12)

The God who watches over sparrows

Before we tally up
every partnered gay man or lesbian
wanting desperately to
answer God's call, let's
remember that God tallies up
every sparrow that flies

or
falls.

Maybe then we'd be
inclined to really
listen to their words
lest we discover to our
sorrow (or worse)
that God has tallied up as well
our denials, now
numbered like the hairs on our head,
each instance we set a
stumbling block to God's call.

(Matthew 10:29-31, Mark 9:42)

Empty barns and bare necks

Said Isaiah (on behalf of God),
the spoils of the poor—and the stoles
of my children,
lesbian and gay—
ended up somehow
neither in their barns nor

laid round their necks;
instead some other
vision than mine dares
even to have stolen what I long to see
stoled.

(Isaiah 3:13-15)

The Goat God

Gladly—gaily?—we cast
about for a scapegoat
to blame our failures on and
hang our fears upon,
ending its life and
redeeming our own;
if only we had
noticed in the tales of our
god, that this One is a

gatherer of goats,
offering sanctuary, welcome,
and even praise to
these we are wont to
stone.

(Isaiah 56:8)

A Palm Sunday Destiny

Such a strange name
our fellow
lutherans cling to,
invoking Peter's confession, no
doubt, yet they end up
rather rocky dirt, a pebbly
obstacle to the seeds
cast by Christ hoping to harvest a whole
kin-dom.

God, be with even these,
our brothers and sisters who
oppose us;
destined, too, are they,
someday with every
other rock and stone, to
intone hosannas to your well-sown
love.

(Matthew 16:18, Mark 4:1-9, Luke 19:39-40)

Praying with Jesus

Kairos means time
in all fullness,
not minutes and hours,
days and years, but
oiled time, anointed by God,
messianic moments.

Come, quickly, dear God,
oil this moment;
make all things kin, now and
ever and ever. Amen.

(Revelation 22:20)

I usually reword the phrase "kingdom of God" as "kin-dom of God" to better capture in a positive form the message and ministry of Jesus. I hint at that here, but more directly suggest that Jesus' original phrase has a quality of deep creative irony to it. His use of "kingdom" does not draw on earthly kings as a metaphor of God; instead, the content of both his parables and his ministry actually use "kingdom" language to severely criticize all earthly manner of holding power. Indeed, given Webster's definition of "queer" as a verb, it is fair to say that Jesus' queers earthly modes of power. The three-part riddle in the fourth verse echoes a Zen koan, giving the disciples (and us) something to ponder after Jesus' death—and a hint at the actions that will resurrect him. I am persuaded that Christian claims about resurrection ought not be metaphysical claims about a body in a tomb 2000 years ago but rather ethical claims about how we honor the Body of Christ today.

29. The Queer Kingdom of God
(July 22, 2005)

Said Jesus to those gathered near, "The kingly deeds of God are queer—
They foul the plans of those whose more is but the spoils of the poor.
God's kingly deeds intend to spoil earth's foolish dreams of what is royal.
The tales I tell are meant to free your ears to hear, your eyes to see
When God is king the rule of men is plain no rule at all, my friends.
When wealth and power go hand in hand, 'tis tyranny that leads the land.

"Thus God does queer the very thing that earth imagines makes a king;
It isn't wealth or might or name, not brutal force or far-flung fame.
The royalty of God begins by claiming every person kin.
When God is king and claiming kin, the outcast ones are gathered in.
No wonder then that under breath the pow'rs that be now whisper death
To One who dares to call their bluff, suggest they've ruled for long enough.

"For regal claims of welcome wide the Christ of God is crucified.
But let this riddle hold you then, that kin-dom come might come again.
'What is the sound of mustard seed growing wild like a weed?
What is the sound of leavened wheat, flour stretched for all to eat?
What is the sound of new made wine, bursting skins of old design?'

"To enemies, speak now as friends, and with the poor make full amends.
Let kindness be the name you chase so every stranger finds a place.
Let welcome be the wealth you keep, and keep it well, both wide and deep.
The doing of these holy deeds—this sounds like wine and wheat and seeds,
For resurrection will begin when you join God in making kin."

The following five pieces all anticipate or reflect on the 2005 Churchwide Assembly of the Evangelical Lutheran Church in America. It seemed almost possible that change might occur in the voting. It did not, but something just as significant did happen (see "Margin to Center") and everything after Orlando will be marked by what took place there.

30. Calling Down Fire
(August 1, 2005)

With the approach of the ELCA Churchwide Assembly, Goodsoil, the alliance of Lutheran organizations working for full participation of GLBT persons in the Lutheran church, has asked friends across the country—indeed around the globe—to fashion a seamless web of prayer, a continuous prayerful vigil throughout the Assembly. This is good.

But, my friends, I believe we can—and must—go a step further. If we focus our prayers with simple yet meaningful ritual, our focused energy will become a doorway through which God's full liberating light will come streaming in. I am not talking about magical incantation. Rather, as Bishop Hanson suggests, I urge us to "be the Body of Christ" with so much conviction in these days that God's longing for justice, which always has been and always will be, is given the full benefit of our invitation to *be now.* I am talking about an intentional effort to call down fire upon Orlando—to petition God for Pentecost in August.

Whether you formally participate in Goodsoil's prayer vigil or simply keep prayerful watch with the Assembly each day on your own, I ask that all of us focus the form of our prayer in the following ways. These tangible elements will help us incarnate—embody—our longing for justice, blending our passion with God's passion until the two become one.

On Monday, August 8, whenever and however you pray, begin this Assembly in advent, in deep expectation. Begin with a flame. Light a match, a candle, an oil lamp, a fireplace, a bonfire, a mattress (but be careful!). On Monday, around the globe, let there be a conflagration of flames big and small, near and far. Pray that God will lighten the darkness that holds this church in fear.

124

On Tuesday, August 9, whenever and however you pray, move this Assembly into Christmas/Epiphany. Splash water and remember your baptism. Dip your fingers and cross yourself, take a gulp and quench your thirst, take a bath, go swimming. On Tuesday, let the waters of the world join our plea. Pray that, as Jesus became the first Body of Christ, this Assembly will at last recognize in us, marked forever with the cross of Christ, fellow members of the present Body of Christ.

On Wednesday, August 10, whenever and however you pray, move this Assembly into Lent. Find some ash and make a cross on your forehead, whether for all day or for all of a minute. Use palm ash or make some ash of your own. Use cigarette ash or oven soot if you must. But on Wednesday, let every friend of full participation be ash-crossed as a symbol of penitence on behalf of this church—*and* as a sign of Jesus' resolute readiness to go to Jerusalem, come what may. Imagine an Assembly speckled with ashes on Wednesday! Pray that this church will repent and that we will follow Jesus all the way to Jerusalem.

On Thursday, August 11, whenever and however you pray, move this Assembly into Holy Week/Easter. As Goodsoil gathers in Orlando for a Thursday evening Eucharist, under the theme "Celebrate the Promise . . . Pour Out the Spirit," join us in bread and wine. Attend a satellite worship service in your area (see www.goodsoil.org). Break some bread and pour some wine. Either in formal Eucharist or in casual conviviality, toast the justice of Jesus and taste the goodness of God's grace. On Thursday, around the globe, let wheat and wine *again* usher in the kin-dom of God. Pray that the gracious welcome of God be tasted by every voting delegate as their lives are caught up in the liturgical drama of our own.

On Friday, August 12 (the first possible day of an Assembly vote on sexuality matters), whenever and however you pray, move this Assembly into the Day of Pentecost! To be messianic is to be anointed, *to be smeared with oil.* Oil this moment early today. Find some liturgical oil, use some body oil, smear some vegetable or olive or peanut oil if necessary. But pray today with oiled fingertips. Ask God to make this moment a messianic moment, chosen for the revealing of God's love. Let Friday morning be a morning that slides into noon in oily anticipation of good news.

125

On Saturday, August 13 (another possible day for an Assembly vote on sexuality matters), whenever and however you pray, move this Assembly into the Season of Pentecost, the Time of the Church. Find a rock, a pebble, a boulder, and touch it while you pray. Remember both the stone that Pilate foolishly thought could stop the message and ministry of Jesus and also the folly of those calling themselves Solid Rock who today seek to stop the Body of Christ from taking on fresh life in our full inclusion. On Saturday, whether in anticipation of a vote yet to come, or in celebration/lament of a vote already taken, in every place that we are, let the rocks and stones carry our voice heavenward. Whether we are jubilant or tearful, on this day, touching rocks and stones, let our prayers sing hosanna for freedom that is already ours, regardless of this church's choice to sing with us, but with fervent hope that it will (and remember that this hope is less for our sake than for this church's).

On Sunday, August 14, as the Assembly concludes, whenever and however you pray, move this Assembly once again into Advent, into full anticipation of the Coming of Christ. Grab some dirt. Let it be rich loam or dry sand, hard clay or caked dust. It doesn't matter, because *in God's care all soil is good soil*. Hold this dirt in your hands as you pray. Water it with your tears, whether of joy or grief. A vote in our favor only begins our work in a new direction. A vote against us only deepens the guilt of this church and renews our work in greater earnest. In either case, we—each one of us—is a person of good soil, of rich promise. On this day, pray simply in the deep spirit of advent, *"Maranatha!* Come quickly, Lord Jesus. Come quickly!"

Understand me. I am not suggesting that these small gestures will somehow guarantee us "victory." But I am saying this: that if we together focus our prayerful energy in this embodied fashion *we will unleash fire in Orlando*. Not by wielding any magical power, but by communally, in a united chorus, opening ourselves to and immersing our prayerful longing in the deep longing of God's own heart. If we do this, from near to far, from Florida to Alaska and beyond, we will not fail to find ourselves aflame with the fire of God. What the church does with us in that event is its own affair. What God does with us in that event is nothing less than Pentecost.

Please, join with me in calling down fire in Orlando in August. Make this an oiled moment. Now. Amen.

31. From Margin to Center: Holding Our Ground
(August 14, 2005)

In the Palms Ballroom at the Marriott Hotel, the 1000+ voting delegates for the ELCA Churchwide Assembly were seated at tables in the center two-thirds of the room. At either end of the room two wide swaths of seats held another couple hundred registered visitors. And at the outer edges of everything, in two single lines, we stood—about 20 of us at a time at each edge—in silent vigil. At times wearing stoles given by (or in honor of) gay and lesbian persons called to ministry but removed from their calls or denied the opportunity to answer them in the first place, we were barely noticeable. We were less than 2% of the people in the room. And the dais and video screens were positioned so that the voting delegates would never even notice that we were there *unless they looked to the margins.* But we were there. At the margins, standing in "stolen" silence, bearing witness to stolen voices. We amounted to next to nothing, no more than mustard seeds . . . *scattered on good soil.*

We kept that silent vigil throughout most of the plenary sessions from Monday evening until Friday afternoon. During that time, as hearings and debates were held over resolutions asking that our relationships be blessed and that our calls to ministry be honored, we occasionally heard faithful witness to our lives, our loves, and our calls from the Assembly microphones. Yet just as often we heard painful witness to a church held captive not to the gospel but to fear and prejudice, to views of Scripture, tradition, and ecumenism that are not life-giving but life-denying. And we stood, silent, holding our ground.

But on Friday afternoon all of that changed. Following the defeat of a proposed amendment that would have removed all barriers to ordination of gay and lesbian persons, the only resolution remaining on the floor sought to create a second-class tier of clergy in the church. It sought to institutionalize injustice under the guise of generosity and compromise. At that moment, alongside this resolution, *we moved ourselves onto the floor as well.* About 100 members of Goodsoil, the alliance of Lutheran groups working for full participation of GLBT persons in the church, left the visitors gallery and moved quietly, respectfully but quite unmistakably *from margin to center*. Despite the bishop's request that we return to "our place" in the visitor's section, we kept vigil in front of the podium, making uncomfortably clear to the voting delegates that real persons, "marked forever with the cross of Christ," stand—quite literally—at the center of any debate about the fate of our vocations and our lives.

Some persons, including some of our friends and allies, have questioned the wisdom of our actions. They have wondered aloud, sometimes with anguish and frustration, whether our actions set back our cause and whether we alienated persons whose hearts were beginning to soften. This is a real concern, and we need to sit with it for a while. If we wish to model what it means to "journey together faithfully amid disagreement," we must hear these words and let them challenge us. We must also speak to these words and ask that our friends and allies hear us as well.

We took our action thoughtfully, after hours (really months) of deliberation, prayer, and community-building. Every person who entered the Assembly floor had received training on active nonviolence, a posture rooted in the teaching of Jesus and refined in the practice of Gandhi. Each of us had signed a pledge to regard our adversaries as full children of God. We respectfully held our ground despite the bishop's request because our goal was not to demonstrate our good obedience to authority but our resolute faithfulness to the gospel. In the face of this church's efforts over decades—including this most recent "faithful" journey—to keep us in the shadows, to talk about us but not with us, our witness was undeniably disconcerting. And so it had the power to unsettle because it brought to the surface the moral dilemma buried deep in many persons —how dare we treat gay and lesbian persons as though they are ever merely nameless and faceless "behaviors" and "lifestyles"? We took on flesh for the voting delegates, confronting them face to face with our very real humanity. No wonder they felt agitated inside. It is often in moments like this that the Holy Spirit births new awareness in persons, new capacity for empathy, for compassion, for justice. This moment of agitation, a moment of *kairos* in biblical terms, sits at the heart of active nonviolence. As participants in this action we made the audacious choice to play midwife to God's longing for justice, seeking to create a moment in which God might do a new thing in the hearts of others in the Assembly hall.

It is certainly debatable whether we accomplished that, but I think there is evidence to suggest that we did. More than a few of the voting delegates wept while we kept our vigil. Many hymnals were brought forward and shared with us during the singing. Countless hugs were offered to us afterwards. And I know that not all of these tears and hugs and hymnals came from our strong allies. At least some of these came from our adversaries—moved in this moment to do some thing new. Perhaps most significantly, in the immediate context of our defiant witness the Assembly still refused by a healthy majority to call for a firm enforcement of Vision & Expectations. In the very moment when they had most reason to legislate us back into hiding (as if that were possible!) they did not. Altogether it seems to me a moment of decisive victory though not measurable on any voting machine.

We can debate our success further, but any debate should be framed with a clear understanding of the principles of nonviolence. Obviously, we crossed the boundaries of "Minnesota nice" that colors much of the Lutheran landscape quite beyond the shores of Lake Woebegone, but we must not forget that Jesus crossed those boundaries so regularly that they collected the tales of his boundary crossings and made them into a set of books that we call gospel—good news.

Finally, I want to suggest that as Lutherans we have a unique resource for appreciating the power of nonviolent action. Luther's theology of the cross, responsible for the Lutheran love affair with "paradox," makes this daring claim: that God is most clearly revealed and fully present in deep vulnerability, and that in Jesus we are shown that weakness is not the absence of power but the doorway through which God's presence moves. As we stood, making calm eye contact with the voting delegates, *we stood at the foot of the cross.* And, my friends, God stood there with us. We held our ground—"like trees planted by the waters," *we could not be moved.* As we stood there for nearly three hours, unarmed, unthreatening, unspeaking, simply and vulnerably present to our brothers and sisters, *we were the theology of the cross made incarnate.*

129

In "Calling Down Fire," my pre-Assembly meditation, I wrote, "What the church does with us in that event [of faithful witness] is its own affair. What God does with us in that event is nothing less than Pentecost." You will not read it in the newspaper accounts, but ask any one of us on the floor yesterday afternoon, and you will hear: we "were all together in one place. And suddenly a sound came from heaven like the rush of a mighty wind, and it filled all the house where they were sitting." Our liturgical calendar is off this year. *Pentecost came on August 12, 2005.*

This church, including some of our deepest adversaries and some of our dearest friends, is feeling off balance right now. I will hazard a guess why. Something transpired in Orlando that none of us could have predicted. It happened because of the legislative work done, the votes cast, the vigils kept, the messages handed out, the lines crossed, the ground held, and most especially because of the God who came to keep us company. We did not get the legislative victories we had hoped far. But more than ever before, in the very midst of a church that continues to disempower us, *we claimed our power and held onto it.* If many of us are a little off balance today, I suspect it is because we have lived so long—really all of our lives, every last one of us—in a church clouded on this issue by unabating darkness, *and so our eyes were not prepared for the first strong glint of the coming dawn.*

A reflection as the Assembly ended.

32. When Worship Wounds
(August 14, 2005)

The vast majority of GLBT persons and their allies who gathered in Orlando last week left incredibly empowered. Our witness to each other and to the ELCA was joyful and energized. Our voices at the mic were many and eloquent; our votes, though not yet victorious, were strong. So there is much cause to be hopeful about our work. Assembly worship, however, was not a cause for celebration . . .

All week long at the ELCA Churchwide Assembly, worship has been a moment of stark irony. Our hymns and our liturgical responses have been rich with images of welcome, justice, and inclusion. But not once in any prayer, responsive reading, or sermon have the words "gay and lesbian persons" been uttered. *Not once!* This was so despite the fact that no other matter commanded even a fraction of the Assembly time devoted to deciding exactly what the Church meant by its pledge to welcome us into its life in resolutions not once but three times (Churchwide Assemblies 1991, 1995, 1999).

But from the moment I saw the First Lesson assigned for our closing worship (Isaiah 56:1, 6-8), I knew this service would be especially brutal for us. We had just finished an Assembly in which our committed relationships and our vocational calls were yet again pushed to the margins, unrecognized by our church and denied full authenticity in the eyes of God. What anguish then to hear these words read at the center of our closing worship: "Thus says the Lord God, who gathers the outcasts of Israel, I will gather others to them besides those already gathered." Did those in worship cringe that they had one more time refused to be part of God's gathering activity? Was there a knot in their stomachs to match the one in ours? Were their cheeks wet, as many of ours were, at another missed opportunity for homecoming?

Our anguish only deepened at the reading of the Gospel (Matthew 15:21-28). It was good news indeed, but good news wounds deeply when practice does not match proclamation. We listened as Jesus was challenged by

131

a plea for recognition from a Canaanite woman, a person with no recognized worth in his society. After a moment of hesitation Jesus stepped across centuries of bias and boundary and met her simply and wholly on the ground of her faith, saying, "Woman, great is your faith! Let it be done for you as you wish." Did those in worship realize that they had just finished refusing to meet us simply and wholly on the ground of our faith, insisting instead that our sexuality—like her Canaanite heritage—be the defining feature of our life?

Bishop Roy Riley's sermon challenged us to move beyond comfortable awe at Jesus' healing from a distance (a ministry that our many ELCA mission projects do quite well) to the less comfortable surprise at whom Jesus welcomes into fellowship near at hand. But he stalwartly refused to name gay or lesbians persons directly even once in his message. He preached on texts about the promise of God's surprising welcome—at the conclusion of an Assembly that rejected that welcome for gay and lesbian persons—and he never once invited the congregation to consider that appalling contradiction.

Our lives were erased, not only from the legislative action of this Assembly but even from its worship life. Some will say, of course, that to have named us in a sermon, or to have prayed for us, or even to have prayed for the church as it encountered us, would have "politicized" worship. But Jesus' central metaphor for the activity of God is political: he proclaimed the "kingdom of God" because his message and ministry revealed the way God builds community, grounded on a politics of radical welcome and deep compassion. For this church to choose not to mention us a single time in its seven (!) Assembly worship services was a profoundly political use of worship. It invited the entire Assembly to erase us from any place in their prayerful consideration of how to build the community of God in this time and place. Taken as a whole, these worship services evidence not simply a lack of welcome for gay and lesbian persons in the life of this church, *they evidence our abandonment.*

132

33. Only a Matter of Time Now?
(August 14, 2005)

I am among those who are, as I told one person, "solemnly ecstatic" about what happened at the ELCA Churchwide Assembly in Orlando. Not because of what the Assembly did. It didn't do much. It refused to endorse blessings for same-sex couples in committed relationships. But it also refused to explicitly ban them. It refused to remove the barriers to the ordination of persons in covenanted same-sex relationships who also find themselves called to ministry. But it also refused to strengthen the threat of discipline against pastors and churches who journey faithfully into such a call. And it refused to create an exceptional call process for such persons, which would have resulted in an institutionalized system of second-class clergy.

Some might say the church chose unity, but I don't think anyone on any side really feels very united. Like a dysfunctional family, we just barely avoided airing our dirtiest laundry in public, but by now all the neighbors know our smiling faces are a façade. *The church chose mediocrity.* It chose to be something less than the people of God, something more akin to the anxious steward, eager to return the church to God exactly as received. Never mind that the parable does not heap high praise on this particular servant; it is at least a model of (mediocre) faithfulness drawn from the Bible.

Of course, one can mine the votes for various glimmers of hope, and both sides will try to spin the numbers to claim the clear momentum is on their side. I suspect that the stronger reading rests on the side of full inclusion, if for no other reason than that the press of society (which, sadly, is too often the backdoor through which the Spirit must blow into the church these days) is with us. But my real hope lies elsewhere.

My confidence for the future, and for a future that will come sooner rather than later, rests in what happened at Orlando among those "on the sidelines," among those who came not to vote but to hold vigil. Our numbers were larger than ever before, our tactics were more daring than ever before, our energy was more focused and coordinated than ever before. *In our souls we turned a corner, and while victory is not yet ours, we know that we will never again be pushed into the shadows.* Not in worship and not in legislation. And I daresay the Church (even if with some bitterness over our tactics) knows this, too. We have decisively shifted the balance of power. Not to say that we have tried to assume control ourselves or that we have even leveled the playing field. But we have acted *with power*—and held our ground, even when the Church tried to scold us back into submission. *We have become a soulforce.*

So, I say with deep confidence, with a solemnly ecstatic mood, that it is only a matter of time now. But before any of us, allies especially, think we can simply wait it out, I need to remind us that it is most surely *not* "only a matter of time." Perhaps now we can project that the cases of depression, attempted and completed suicides, shattered families, shattered faiths, collapsed relationships and ruptured calls will reach "only" into the thousands before Lutherans make real the welcome they promised more than a decade ago. But no good Lutheran or Christian or person will be comforted by that.

As long as the injustice of our church exacts such a devastating toll on our people, our confidence will be at once jubilant and tireless. It has *never* been "only a matter of time." It has always been—and remains even now—a matter of life and death. And we must daily imagine and then make choices that preserve and promote the fullness of life as swiftly as we can.

34. Marked Forever with the Ambiguity of the Church
(August 17, 2005)

"We're going to Orlando to be the Body of Christ!" proclaimed Mark Hanson on behalf of the ELCA. With the 2005 Churchwide Assembly over, it seems we went there to *wound* the Body of Christ instead.

Four times now (1991, 1995, 1999, 2005) the ELCA has officially welcomed gay and lesbian persons into the life of the church. According to this year's theme, they too, are "marked with the cross of Christ forever." Yet since its inception in 1988, the ELCA has added an asterisk for homosexuals: "marked forever," yes, but regardless of personal piety, Christ-centered theology, confessional commitment, biblical understanding, or ethical integrity, this church believes their sexuality somehow marks them more deeply than the cross of Christ. Spoken aloud that claim would be heresy; in practice, however, it passes for good church policy.

I was in Orlando with Goodsoil, the alliance of Lutheran groups pressing for full participation for gay and lesbian persons. If we appeared at times weary, weeping, even wounded, it was because we embodied what was being done to the Body of Christ.

Worship was painful. As our lives hung in the balance of Assembly deliberation, no prayer, responsive reading, or sermon ever spoke the word gay or lesbian—in any of the seven Assembly worship services. Liturgy, song, and sermon abounded with justice; Sunday's final worship texts highlighted God's welcome to persons long considered outcast. But the absence of our names invited anyone who wished, to imagine us outside the claims of God, outside the reach of this justice. Aiming to avoid any appearance of "politicizing worship" by praying for the very people it claims to welcome, the church instead politicized worship by abandoning them in the sanctuary while debating them in the plenary. We wept on Sunday morning as much for the church as for ourselves.

135

The Assembly voted overwhelmingly to continue in a "unity" that is increasingly violent toward and toxic to many gay and lesbian persons. Like a dysfunctional family that denies the abuse that distorts it, we voted to stay together for more of the same.

The Assembly was decisively ambiguous about whether gay and lesbian relationships, so deeply blessed by God, might also receive the church's blessing—"decisively," because multiple amendments to specifically ban or endorse such blessings failed. The church promised "pastoral care," with intended ambiguity, to the same persons it claims unambiguously to "welcome into its life."

The Assembly defeated a resolution to create a separate process of ordination for selected gay and lesbian persons. Hailed by some as a step forward, a gracious gesture of compromise, it offered a "two-door" ordination process, with one door marked "queers use this entrance." Under the guise of progress it would have institutionalized a failure to discern the Body of Christ.

When nothing more than second-class citizenship was left on the floor for consideration, 100 members of Goodsoil moved themselves onto the voting floor for consideration as well. Peacefully, respectfully, silently. But we were quite visible, and the Assembly's agitation at our presence was palpable. Some called us "intimidating." Imagine 100 African-American persons taking the floor during an all-white Assembly in the 60's; no matter the peacefulness of their demeanor, they would've been perceived as intimidating for the same reasons we were. We embodied the "other" that many in the Assembly hall feared. And we embodied it in the very moment that they wanted us to be patiently invisible so they could discuss our fate without seeing our eyes.

I have heard that our full welcome is "only a matter of time" and that we actually hurt our own cause by "disrupting" the Assembly. This charge fails to hold in the balance the countless depressions, shattered families, collapsed relationships, lost faiths, and suicides, by which this church has disrupted our lives and wounded the Body of Christ. To have stood silently in the visitors section while the church yet again proclaimed welcome while inflicting wounds would have been to deny Jesus as truly as Peter denied him by the campfire. "Surely, you, too, were with him, for I see the mark of Christ on your forehead." And, for us, in that moment there was no other choice but to say, "Yes," with all our hearts and with all our feet moving from the margins of this church to the center. From now on this conversation is not about us. *It is us. We, too, are the Body of Christ.*

I wrote this short piece during the early spring of 2006 when "Minnesota Nice" (yet again) got drawn into the national fascination with proposing amendments to state constitutions making any legal recognition of same-sex marriages virtually impossible. In Minnesota, thus far, we've had plenty of grandstanding but (thankfully!) nothing on the ballot.

35. Sunday School . . . and the Politics of Marriage
(March 2006)

It sure seems like God is awful busy politicking these days. While no one is clamoring to erase the boundary between church and state, the debate in many states over amendments to ban same-sex marriage has kept God's calendar of speaking engagements full all spring.

People of faith—Christians mostly—are eager to bring God into Capital rotundas of late, both on posters and at podiums. As a result, in the last round of elections fifteen states added amendments effectively banning same-sex marriage, bringing the total of states with such amendments to eighteen. At least seven, and perhaps as many as seventeen more states will put such amendments before their voters this fall.

God (or at least the posters and speakers who claim to know God's will on this) almost always weighs in against same-sex marriage and in favor of constitutional amendments on top of laws already in place to doubly insure that this particular piece of the divinely designed social fabric cannot be unraveled. But occasionally, God makes a guest appearance for the other side. That's when things begin to get interesting. It's no longer my word against yours, but God's word . . . against God's.

As someone largely sitting on the sidelines of this debate—I am, after all, straight, happily married, and plenty busy parenting five kids—I can't help but wonder how God feels about being caught in this political tug of war.

Well, I don't exactly sit on the sidelines. To be honest, I'm a devout Christian man. In fact, I'm so dedicated to raising the next generation of children with solid Christian values that I have stepped forward to do what few Christian men dare to do: teach 3rd and 4th grade Sunday School. It's a humbling endeavor to match my calm wisdom against the ever incipient pandemonium of my 3rd and 4th graders. But I will say this, I love them dearly, and I am determined to safeguard the world that I will bequeath to them all too soon.

Zinash (a bright-eyed 9-year old girl adopted from Ethiopia only a year ago) has won my heart. Not long ago in Sunday School we were studying the Christian creed. We encouraged each child to put the faith they held into their own simple words. Zinash's four-sentence creed was eloquent even though she is still working on her English: "I believe in God who make everything. I believe in Jesus who came to earth. I believe in the church because it teach me about God. I believe in my moms because she will always love me."

The last sentence is grammatically wrong, but it's the one that helps explain where I take my stand on this issue. The error isn't that Zinash pluralized "moms"; it's that she forget to use "they" instead of "she." Zinash has *two* moms, a lesbian couple who adopted her and her younger brother after they were orphaned by AIDS in 2003. In fact, if I look over my Sunday School roster, four of my nine kids have same-sex parents in their lives. Four of the nine children who look to me to tell them something about the God who loves them have learned the first lesson of that love from same-sex parents.

I don't imagine those statistics are true in many Sunday School classes, but they are the gospel truth in mine (and at my church they are pretty much the norm from pre-school through confirmation). Zinash and her classmates seem to take something for granted about the God of the Bible that's often forgotten on the posters and unspoken at the podiums: *this God has a knack for including people that the insiders would rather leave outside.*

In the Bible, Ruth, a Moabite woman—a member of a people cursed in the Bible—becomes a metaphor for God's faithfulness. Isaiah surprises the people of his day by announcing that foreigners—previously forbidden any place in the assembled people of God because they were regarded as unclean—actually have an honored spot in the family, and that their praise finds a special place in the heart of God. Jonah explains that the only thing worse in his mind than doing time in the belly of a whale is having to watch God show mercy on people he (Jonah) detests.

Meanwhile, in the New Testament, in one of the most famous parables recorded in Luke's gospel, Jesus uses a Samaritan—the most despised person in Jewish society—as an image for God's compassion. And in Acts, Peter is stunned to see Cornelius—an unclean, uncircumcised Gentile—experience the baptism of the Holy Spirit before the early church had even discussed, let alone approved his baptism by water.

So perhaps it isn't all that surprising that in my Sunday School class, I find Zinash teaching me something today about God and the politics of marriage. She reminds me that God's love never has been and never will be confined to a "preferred" set of people. It's always reaching out to those at the margins—often in ways that make the rest of us nervous.

Yes, it may seem like God is busy politicking these days—but I'm not at all convinced that it's God who's doing the politicking on most of the posters or at most of the podiums. God's politics are far less predictable than human prejudice. Alice Walker said famously in The Color Purple, "I think it pisses God off if you walk by the color purple in a field somewhere and don't notice it." Well, listening to my own 3rd and 4th graders in Sunday school, I have to say that I think it also pisses God off when we walk by the beauty of love in our world and don't notice it—or worse, try to amend constitutions to make sure no one ever notices it.

I wrote this talk for the 2006 Lutherans Concerned/North America Biennial Assembly, Together in Toronto: Claiming an Open Spirit. I was part of a panel on "Queering the Bible," in which several of us shared thoughts on more promising methods of biblical interpretation.

36. Leaning into the Text with our Lives: A People's Approach to the Bible
(August 2006)

It is 1:30 p.m. on Tuesday. In exactly 24 hours I will board a greyhound bus in St. Paul, Minnesota and travel with my beloved Margaret to Toronto, where I will say who-knows-what to all of you.

"Who-knows-what" because so far five drafts of this presentation are on my virtual desktop virtually crumpled up. I have just returned from an hour-long walk in the hot sun. Perhaps hoping that heat stroke will suffice for further inspiration.

I have with me a few freshly frazzled thoughts that I scribbled in a spiral notebook while I strolled, and I have made my way up to J & S Bean Factory, where I am praying—yes, literally praying—that the ambiance of this neighborhood coffee shop will take the edge off my edginess and let the words flow.

On the way in I greet the owner, Erika, and in reply to her casual inquiry, I offer a bald-faced lie: "I'm fine." However, I decide that putting this lie out into the universe is hardly the way to invite good karma toward my keyboard. So, while she prepares my drink, a mixed berry granita (sort of a high-brow slushy) I confess, "Actually, I'm feeling pretty frantic." I explain that all of you are waiting for me to say who-knows-what and that I'm fast slipping into deep woe-is-me anxiety. Erika smiles and offers words of reassurance, mostly drowned out by the blender. But I do hear the word "grace" come through. And as the blender quiets down, I catch her last sentence: "Plus, of course, it's all much bigger than just you and me," she says, smiling. Then she adds, "Your drink is on the house today—in gratitude for the work you do."

Simple kindness. Erika's shop is one of the most grace-full places I know. Maybe now my muse will come out to play…

I want offer you a scene from Exodus 3, the well-known tale of the burning bush. Moses is in the wilderness, tending sheep when his curiosity is piqued by a seemingly ordinary bush ablaze with a fire that does not consume it. More amazing still, out of the bush comes a Voice that not only promises liberation for Moses and his people, but also insists that Moses himself, over his strong objections, will play a role in bringing about that liberation.

This Voice finally names Itself at Moses' request. Although sometimes interpreted as the evasion of a name, really the name fits this God who promises liberation better than any other name could. Often in the Bible names are the footholds that allow us to stand in relationship with the person named. Moses' wants to know how to be in relationship with this Voice. And God—after promising to free a group of slaves, lead them to a land, provide for their life, and be their God—God says, "If you want to be in relationship with me, remember that my name is YHWH: I will be who I will be."

The name tells Moses at least two things. This is a God whose divinity is rooted in making and fulfilling promises; nothing more than this needs to be said. Except for this one thing more: this is a God who will not be boxed in by any limitation on the way to fulfilling those promises. This God can promise liberation because this God is Liberation, not as a concept, but as an activity, as a divine energy now directing Itself toward these people in this moment.

That's the scene. My intent is not so much to walk through it as a text—although that is surely worth doing—but rather to share some thoughts on how to approach Scripture that have emerged for me as I have lived with this scene. I've titled my reflections, "Leaning into the Text with our Lives: A People's Approach to the Bible." I suppose you could call it a "Communal Participatory Liberationist Hermeneutic," but that seems a bit clumsy.

So I will identify seven essential facets of how I think a whole people might approach Scripture well, with hope, power, and integrity. Seven is a lot, I know, but I really believe each one is essential. Something gets lost if any of them is left out.

First, *your life*. When I suggest that we "lean into the text with our lives," I mean that we must claim the full authority of our lived, embodied experience. Our lives—our joy and grief, our hope and despair, our daily rhythms and our sublime ecstasies—all of this is an arena in which God is active. The biblical text is the result of people daring to claim such authority for their lived experiences long past. It is time for us to claim such authority for our lived experience today. And with that lived experience to lean into the biblical text. I do not say that our individual lives always have final authority; we are certainly capable of being mistaken. But our lives are texts into which God does venture, and when we acknowledge this, we will be able to meet the biblical text as a partner in a conversation about God across time and place. It will be a conversation sometimes marked by agreement and sometimes by disagreement; sometimes by confusion and sometimes by discovery. But it will be a conversation that is richer, fuller, *and more revelatory* when our lives become part of it.

Second, *community*. I said "your life" a moment ago, because there is no generic, general lived experience. There is only *your* experience. For each one of you. We are, each one of us, utterly unique. And yet we do this leaning into the text best as a community venture, as a People's approach. Just as the authors of the biblical text, we, too, have biases and blind spots. We, too, are capable of imagining our personal prejudices as prophetically visionary. And we, too, are prone to read the misfortunes of life as personal judgments against us. And the best guard we have against either of these extremes is the company of each other. Thus, the best way to engage the Bible in theological conversation is in the company of others. I know it isn't always convenient. Sometimes it isn't even possible. But, honestly, the Bible is a community book, and we—together—are part of its community. I think that's true for all Christians, but for those of us who have often found the Bible used in damaging ways against us, we have all the more reasons—to protect ourselves from either arrogance or despair—to venture into its pages together.

Third, *claim the text as witness to gracious liberation and welcome*. The Bible can be made to say many things. Any good biblical theology will recognize that the (small 'w') words of the Bible are human etchings that seek to bear witness to the (big 'W') Word of God. The weight of any particular biblical text is measured by its capacity to bear witness to the (big 'W') Word. The technical term for this is "canon within the canon." It is the honest recognition that the Bible does not speak with one voice and that we have no choice but to make a faithful claim about where we hear God's Voice among the many voices that cross its pages. Part of the challenge here is that most of us are trained to hear the Voice of God in a particular way—and in what is seldom a particularly life-giving way—long before we notice what's happening. Just as many of us internalize shame about homosexuality before we realize we've internalized shame about ourselves, many of us internalize a Voice of God that speaks primarily in rules, demands, and judgment before we ever realize that were other Voices we might have preferred to internalize. This is a sometimes long but utterly essential transformation of perspective. Listen carefully, *we must be able to confess that the Voice among the voices, the Word among the words, belongs to a God whose deepest Self is gracious liberation and welcome.* Until we can enter the text to speak with *this* God, we are better off not to enter it all. Every Christian makes a choice about the Voice that holds trump value in the Bible. We must be exceptionally clear about the Voice we place our trust in.

Fourth, *participatory.* The God we encounter in the Bible is (or ought to be) a God of gracious liberation and welcome. But just as importantly, this God expects us to participate. In the momentous scene with the Burning Bush, God promises a whole new future to the Hebrews, but God also asks Moses to play a leading role. And while the psalmist might sing about the Lord bearing the people up on eagle's wings, there were undoubtedly a lot more callused feet than feathered wings involved in the Exodus. So this gracious liberation and welcome isn't a promise that we passively receive, it's a promise that we claim by participating in its unfolding. And that is not only an important theological observation, it is also an essential aspect of how we read the Bible. *This is not someone else's story; it's yours.* The biblical text reads differently once you have chosen to become an active participant in the gracious liberation and welcome it promises.

Fifth, *outward-moving, other-oriented.* This promise of gracious welcome and liberation is absolutely made to you. But it is *also* absolutely made to everyone else still longing for freedom and welcome. We don't get to keep this promise to ourselves. And the moment we do, it acts like hoarded manna: it gets sticky and foul-smelling. Another important theological observation, that is also an essential aspect of how we read the Bible. This is not just your story; it's a story seeking to gather others into it as well. And the biblical text reads differently once you have chosen to become an active participant in the gracious liberation and welcome it promises to *others besides yourself*.

Sixth, *poetic and creative*. When we lean into the text with our lives we will have unexpected moments of insight. We will see places where our lives, our experiences, our embodiment, touch the text with fresh insight. But this will happen more often if we can see the places where this touching happens indirectly, evocatively, but often still very profoundly. All of us are capable of noticing these places of subtle touch, but often we are blessed if there is a poetic voice in the company with whom we read (or in our library) to help us see these connections. Something similar is true when we read the Bible as participants in the promise of widening and gracious welcome and liberation. Because we are continuing this story in the texts of our own lives, we must read with a particular readiness to be surprised, with a particular creative spirit to see where new pathways to and fresh possibilities for liberation and welcome lie.

Seventh: *open-ended*. It goes without saying, and yet it must be said because the Christian tradition has an unhappily consistent record of thinking that *this time* it has given the biblical text a definitive reading once and for all. *No.* Every time a new life or new experience is brought into the conversation the reading will be different. Every time a new manner of oppression appears—or a new moment of liberation is realized—the reading will be different. Patterns will emerge, yes. But it seems clear to me that God preferred the tabernacle to the Temple as a dwelling, because the Tabernacle walls could billow with the Wind. We should always read the Bible with a breeze in the room just to remind us of the billowing Wind.

I call this "A People's Approach to the Bible" because it isn't scholarly or specialized. It's communal, public, and participatory. We need the best creative scholarship we can find, but just as much we need models that enable us to meet the Bible as we are and as it is. I hope this model makes a contribution in that direction, empowering us to "lean into the biblical text with our own lives."

I was invited to preach at St. Paul-Reformation Lutheran Church (where I am a member) the Sunday before the start of the 2007 Evangelical Lutheran Church in America (ELCA) Churchwide Assembly. During this week-long national Assembly delegates would again consider whether to allow lesbian and gay persons in committed relationships to have their relationships blessed in church ceremonies and whether such persons in committed same-sex relationships can serve as ordained pastors in the ELCA. Hopes were high. Lots of strategic planning had preceded the Assembly. But history has shown the ELCA to be very reluctant to lead the way on issues of justice. So, as I ascended the pulpit steps, who knew whether this week would end in celebration or lament? My task as preacher was to offer hope that could not be easily deflated by the whims of a historically timid denomination, words to keep my friends in the pew good company in the week that lay ahead.

37. Clothed in Christ
(August 5, 2007)

According to the liturgical calendar, we're in that part of the church year called "ordinary time." But today is no ordinary Sunday. Tomorrow the ELCA Assembly begins in Chicago. And by next Sunday our life in the ELCA, as individuals and as a congregation might be profoundly different . . . or it might be pretty much the same.

This year's theme for the Assembly is "Living in God's Amazing Grace," but who can say whether the ELCA will choose this year to extend any of that "amazing grace" to us?

In today's Gospel reading (Luke 12:13-21), beyond the warning about building bigger barns in order to keep all that we have to ourselves, we hear Jesus urge us to be rich toward God instead. And in today's epistle (Colossians 3:1-11), as I explained to the children in the children's sermon, we are encouraged to dress ourselves in attitudes and actions that reflect our life in Christ.

So, I'm going to offer seven words of wisdom this morning as we gather with the Assembly looming ahead of us. Words to keep us focused on being rich toward God. Words to keep us clothed with Christ. Words to keep near to your hearts and minds as the week unfolds—come what may.

First: In one very real sense *the votes don't matter at all.* This is perhaps the most important thing to keep in mind as each day unfolds. There will be votes on rules and on which pieces of legislation to deal with. There may be votes on blessings and ordinations and discipline—or these matters may be silenced, referred to committees. In dysfunctional families, the preferred way to "live together faithfully" is often to faithfully silence the voices that seek change.

But we must be very clear—for our own spiritual well-being: the ELCA does *not* get to vote on either our welcome or our worth. In the ELCA, as in any gathered community of God, *worth is God's to give and welcome is God's to declare.* At best, even a positive vote on all matters that we care about only affirms a truth that pre-exists the vote itself. Our worth, infinite and unconditional, is not on any ballot. Our welcome, already fully extended by the God who gathers us into God's people, can be acknowledged or hindered by this church but it cannot be undone.

Second: In another very real sense *the votes matter a great deal.* Neither our worth or welcome before God are at stake, yet honesty requires us to recognize that these votes do matter: for us, for our children, for our families and friends, and for our congregations.

This church's willingness (or unwillingness) to refrain from discipline in cases of faithful, prayerful disobedience to the present policy *will* decide how much room the ELCA as an institution allows for God's Wind to blow freely. And that matters.

This church's willingness (or unwillingness) to acknowledge with blessing the joy of our covenanted lives *does* make a difference in the way these relationships are supported in faith communities, in families, in circles of friends, and in conversations about civil rights. To publicly and prayerfully bless a relationship does not add God's blessing—these relationships already enjoy God's blessing—but it does help marshal the gifts of the human community in support of these relationships. And that matters.

This church's willingness (or unwillingness) to affirm calls to ministry that come to GLBT persons from God *will* decide whether to end the rupture between call and community that exists in the Body of Christ today—a rupture that deeply pains those persons in whose lives it occurs and a rupture that weakens all the members of the Body of Christ, even those who say they have no need of us. And that matters.

And, in all these areas, this church's decisions *will* carry the weight—either of God's amazing grace or of humanity's persistent prejudice—far beyond this present place and this present moment. There *will* be persons whose lives will be invited further into the open . . . or driven deeper into the closet. There *will* be persons whose prejudices will be weakened and made less dangerous . . . or made bolder and become more dangerous. There *will* be parents whose capacity to embrace their own children will be deepened . . . or diminished. And there *will* be children just beginning to discover their sexual identity whose ability to love themselves—and to love others—will be affirmed . . . or alienated. And all these things will happen with either holy or devastating consequences. And that matters.

So while nothing in Chicago can determine where we stand with God, much that happens in Chicago will impact where we stand with our brothers and sisters in this church and how we stand as citizens in this society. Our confidence in God's amazing grace should remain unshaken all week, but our celebration or lament, our jubilation or anger, our joy or sorrow is very real and we should embrace it and express it in its fullness.

Third: *We've been here before, so we know (at least in part) what lies ahead—it will not be a walk in the park.*

We know, some of us by heart, the texts that will be turned loose on us like pit-bulls. Texts that rip and tear at our souls because no matter how much you set them in their context somebody else set them in the canon. And they have ever after been available in the arsenal of those who would keep us other than kin.

We know that someone will sound the alarm of "schism"—and then echo the sentiment of Caiaphas, that it is better for this relative handful of queers to be denied full welcome than to anger those who have appointed themselves keeper of that welcome. Never mind that this means lopping us off like limbs from the Body of Christ, failing to see that like Ezekiel's vision of dry bones we are among those whose bones, sinews, and flesh have been knit together into the whole people of God.

We know that someone will hold up their Bible and argue that, out of overwhelming reverence for the leaves of pages in this Book, we must ignore the overwhelming reverence of the lives of gay people in this Body. And ignore as well the biblical witness to a divine freedom that is driven by God's amazing grace and is shown repeatedly to be unlimited by either text or tradition.

And we know that again this year someone and someone and someone else will want more time to study us. To examine our lives, our genes, our environments. Our own ecclesial family will poke, pry, prod, and debate us as though if only we could be thoroughly understood, then all would be resolved. As though the miracle of any particular child of God or that of the entire People of God is grounded in something less than gracious Mystery.

Regardless of how the votes go—or if they go at all—hurtful things will be said. But they may hurt a little less if we remind ourselves that they're coming.

Fourth: *Our bishops have been here, too.* We are not the first people to stand alongside Jesus at the door and knock. Beginning with the messenger sent to Peter from Cornelius, the Holy Spirit has looked to the leaders in the church to model for the whole church the welcome of God that reaches into surprising places and moves among surprising peoples.

When Peter went to meet with Cornelius, there were believers who followed after him precisely because he was a bishop, a public leader in the church. And then all of them together, Peter and those who came with him, saw the Spirit poured out upon Cornelius, a Gentile, and his entire household, in violation of what both text and tradition could have led any of them to expect. And Peter could seize that moment and say to all the faithful that had followed him, "How can our human institution fail to follow the Spirit's holy initiative? Come let us welcome these people, different as they are, as our brothers and sisters in Christ!" The meeting between these early believers and the household of Cornelius happened because a bishop brought other believers with him into an encounter with those whom the early church had not yet welcomed home.

We cannot expect that every bishop will agree with us on every point. But we can expect them—*we can hold them accountable as public leaders in this church*—to insure that still today the faithful 'insiders' are led by our bishops into authentic and genuine encounters with us. Not that fair and balanced conversations are held *about* us, but that genuinely open and prayerful conversations are held *with* us. And in Chicago, as in Joppa and Caesarea, our bishops have a responsibility to lead and to speak, not simply to watch and listen. We have every right to be profoundly pleased or bitterly disappointed with their actions at the Assembly.

Fifth: *There is a difference between worth and integrity.* Thanks to God's amazing grace, there is no question about our worth. But what we hope for, as more and more persons in this church encounter us, is that the integrity of our faith, our love, and our lives—the Christ-clothing we wear—bears witness to our love for God and neighbor.

Thus we aim to echo in our lives the daring compassion that marked Jesus' life. We do this in our bold vision for this congregation and for our larger church as we imagine new ways to meet the world's needs. We do this in the faithful covenants we make to one another, both the personal ones that guide our intimate lives and the public ones that guide our communal lives. We do this in the many creative ways we let compassion move through us throughout the week at work and at home, as consumer and as citizen, as believer and as beloved.

No choice we make can add to our worth in the eyes of God, but every choice we make can impact our integrity before others—so we should attend to these choices well. But let's be very clear: we measure our integrity not by social convention or by ecclesial expectation but by the consistency of our compassion. Doing so lets us determine what we can—our integrity—without thinking that we (or anyone else) can determine our worth.

And, as we move into this particular week, no more powerful prayer can be unleashed on behalf of the widening welcome of God than doing a simple deed of compassion in your daily life. Such prayers are so powerful because they embody our longing in an anticipatory way. If each day this week we attend to the needs and hopes that we encounter in our daily lives—and if we respond as we are able with compassion—our integrity will flourish and we will hold up before God our longing that Grace and Welcome hold sway in this church.

Sixth: At the end of the week, when the dust settles, *this is finally about where Jesus sleeps.* Yes, everything that happens in our regard this week does matter deeply to us. Our congregations and pastors will—or will not—experience restraint in discipline. Our couples will—or will not—have their relationships blessed. Our calls to ministry will—or will not—be confirmed by the church. So at the end of the week our exultation or our anguish will be justified, and it will be real.

But it's important to recognize that *we do not wait upon this church's welcome alone.* As the gospels suggest, "Foxes have holes, birds have nests, and straight people have beds, but until the widening welcome of God is echoed clearly in the policy and practice of this church, Jesus continues to wait wearily for a place to lay his head." Whether the week brings justice and jubilation or more waiting and more wounding, it will make a difference in how we experience this if we recognize it isn't just about us; *it's about Jesus.*

And Seventh: *This is a moment made to be oiled.* This week presents our church with a moment capable of becoming *kairos.* In Greek, *chronos* is time as we usually know it, measured in minutes, hours, days, weeks. *Chronos* is time moving, graciously to be sure but predictably as well, from season to season, year to year, generation to generation. But *kairos* names time measured by fullness, by presence, by promise, by advent. *Kairos* is time made messianic, anointed with oil to serve God's purpose.

This week, then, is a moment made to be oiled. There are no guarantees that it will become so. The biblical witness is painfully poignant in both testaments: the gathered community of God acts with murmuring, stubbornness and rebellion, as often as it acts with faith and daring imagination. No one knows yet—perhaps not even God—what this church will choose to do with this moment of possibility.

But I know this much: that alongside us God longs for this week to be a messianic moment in this church, an occasion anointed for change, an opportune time oiled for holy daring. So I invite each of you this week to keep a little oil close at hand. Perhaps at mealtimes or in the morning and evening, touch your finger to the oil and then feel its hopeful glistening between your fingertips. And simply say, alongside the longing of God: *"May this moment be*

151

oiled for welcome. May this year, this week, be the time when our sisters and brothers can see that we, too, are at home."

This isn't magic. It won't increase our odds. But it will help embody the mystery of our longing. It will help us feel at our fingertips what Jesus came to announce: Behold, the kin-dom of God is at hand.

Seven words to bear in mind, to keep you well-clothed in Christ this week. Now may the ache of God for justice be your ache this week. May the hope of God for reconciliation be your hope this week. And may the joy of God at every deed of compassion be your joy this week. And always.

Amen.

In October 2007 Soulforce and Atticus Circle, two GLBT advocacy groups, sponsored Seven Straight Nights for Equal Rights, a nation-wide series of one-night vigils led by allies during the week of October 7-13. Seven Straight Nights aimed (successfully) to raise media awareness of straight allies who are passionate for GLBT rights, and to fashion a national network of out allies, both longtime and new, who are willing to work in concert for equality. This is an op-ed piece I wrote to help explain why we were doing this here in Minnesota. As the final (most recent) essay in this collection, it fittingly steps from faith convictions into the public square. Our faith is nothing if it fails to be political, if it shies away from seeking to challenge the power structures in our world that are oppressive.

38. Seven Straight Nights
(September 2007)

I came out thirteen years ago. In a church basement. In a circle of people I knew—but not that well. I still remember my heart pounding, my breath catching, my words both desperately trying to get out and desperately trying to stay in. *I was scared.*

This was my moment to speak my truth—or forever regret my silence. But these words, once spoken, would forever change the way my church looked at me. I was scared.

And I was straight.

The week before, discussing homosexuality, person after person voiced their disapproval of "that lifestyle," their discomfort at the thought of worshipping alongside "those kind" of people. I listened as these Christians dehumanized a whole category of people. Gay people (bisexual and trans-gender persons weren't even discussed) were reduced to "the least of these, my brothers and sisters" (Matthew 25:31-46)—but no one was seeing Christ in them at all. I left church carrying the image of my gay and lesbian friends, bruised and bloodied by such "Christian" words, heavy in my heart.

Then—for seven straight nights—I wrestled to find my words. Who was I to speak? My silence cost me nothing. But it was costing my friends everything. And that made it costly to me, too.

The next Sunday, as the discussion became another menacing cascade of fear and prejudice, I noticed that we spoke as if all of "them" were "out there" and our task was to lock and bolt the sanctuary door. Against *them*. But I knew otherwise.

This wasn't about a nameless "them" at all. It was about actual persons—Dale . . . Ruth . . . Paul . . . Kathi . . . Dick . . . Ken—all of them baptized children of God *already in the sanctuary*, just hoping to hear a bit of good news and maybe taste a morsel of it, too. And hoping not to be singled out for condemnation over the very dimension in their lives where they knew the touch of Grace.

That was my moment: between "them" and the names and faces of my friends. Eloquence was not the point, but I wanted words worthy of the faces and lives they held. From scribbled notes, my heart pounding, I stammered: "Time and again I have experienced firsthand God's ability to proclaim good news through the voices and lives of gay and lesbian people. Their sexuality doesn't prevent this. If anything, because of it they have a special kinship with Christ. We, who are straight, like birds, have nests, and like foxes, have dens (Matthew 8:20); they don't—at least not if we can help it.

"But grace has been too real, good news has been far too abundant in their lives for me to believe anything other than that their orientations are a gift from God; and not simply a gift to themselves, but a gift to the whole Church. We fail to discern the very Body of Christ (I Corinthians 11:29) when we fail to see the Grace that moves in their lives next to our own."

Nervous. Scared. Relieved. I was out. And I was surprised by how many people came up to thank me afterwards. There were a lot of timid allies in that church basement, and my stumbling moment of courage brought several of them closer to speaking their own truth.

Since then I've stammered and stumbled my way toward being a louder and more visible ally. I've been blessed beyond words by friendships with GLBT persons—and anguished beyond words each time their dignity and humanity is questioned. *That their lives—and their love—remain marginalized in both civil and faith communities is a mark of neither civility nor faith. It is a dark absence of both, and one into which more and more Allies must step if we would dispel it before our children inherit it.*

For Seven Straight Nights (October 7-13), we aim to do just that. In concert with allies across the country, on Monday night, October 8, in front of the Governor's mansion, we will lift up candles and voices, coming out as allies to say that dignity, humanity—and equality before the law—are the birthright and the measure of a civil society.

To learn more about Seven Straight Nights—and to sign up for the Twin Cities vigil—visit www.sevenstraightnights.org. We'll have a candle lit for you when you arrive.

I've chosen to save this essay for last because it speaks well of a land that has so flowed with milk and honey for me. Written as a keynote message presented to the Unitarian Church in Davenport, Iowa as part of a weekend festival for Quad Citians Active for Diversity, it serves well as an epilogue to the rest of the essays here. I was asked to offer an overview of the major themes in GLBT theology. This is what I came up with.

39. GLBT Theology: A Travelogue and Personal Reflection
(March 30, 2003)

The theme of my message this morning will be "GLBT Theology: A Travelogue and Personal Reflection." I'll begin by briefly explaining my connection to GLBT Theology and then I'll turn to the substance of my thoughts in which I'll offer an overview of the basic insights of GLBT theology and conclude with a few personal reflections.

Most of us, if we are honest, take pretty meandering routes to where we wind up later in life, and my route to GLBT Theology meanders quite a bit. I won't tell you the whole story, but given the ironies of language, I need to say at least this much—as much as my route meanders, it is also *straight*.

So I speak about this theology as something of an outsider. I do not identify myself as gay or lesbian or bisexual or transgender. But as a straight man I have journeyed with wonder, appreciation, and gratitude across the landscape of this theology. And perhaps as a straight person, I can help articulate the promise of this terrain to the larger church.

My connection to this *theology* is through these *people*. Beginning in high school and college, but particularly in seminary, graduate school, and into my first teaching position at Luther College, I came to know enough gay, lesbian, and bisexual persons well as friends that it became impossible for me to consider them—or their love—opposed to God.

As a theologian, it then fell to me not simply to say, "I just know it's okay," but rather to do the study, the reflection, the thinking, the writing, and the speaking to help others see why this could be so.

Ultimately, I entered their land, so to speak, for three reasons, all quite humble. First, in order to be able to better explain them to the rest of us. Second—and perhaps more urgently—I also did this *to be able to better protect them from the rest of us.* And third, because it seemed there were gay, lesbian, bisexual, and ally students at Luther College anxious to visit this theology themselves, and they needed someone to guide them. And so I became their guide to the theology—and they became my guide to the lived experience.

"Us" and "them" are clumsy words. Too easily divisive, but sometimes descriptively honest and inevitable. So let me warn you that while such words are often used to put "us" at an advantage over "them," *when I resort* to these words, by "us" I mean we straight persons who have caused so much suffering and grief for those not like "us." When I say "them," I mean those whose "not-straightness" has made them sexually, culturally, socially, and religiously "the least of these" among whom Jesus pledges to be found. There is no privilege in my "us"; there is usually a tone of confession.

G-L-B-T. Letters can be as clumsy as words. The course I taught at Luther was entitled "Gay & Lesbian Voices in Theology" the first year I offered it. But in the teaching itself I learned how important it is to hear oneself named, so it eventually became "Gay, Lesbian, Bisexual, and Transgender Voices in Theology," which was shortened to a variety of more practical nicknames. Some of the students called it "Pink Theology," a colorful name, but also more "G" than "BLT." Some felt comfortable calling it "Queer Theology"; others felt quite put off by that term. "GLBT Theology" succeeds in "naming" everyone, but does so by reducing everyone to a letter.

How might I sum up the central convictions of GLBT Theology? Well, to begin with, it is multivocal and evolving. It is *multivocal* in that there are many voices within it, and, perhaps in direct response to its own experience of being rendered voiceless for so long, there is a general tendency to allow differing perspectives to sit side-by-side without feeling an urgency to adopt one "orthodox" position. It is *evolving* in that this is relatively young theology, and still unfolding at a pretty fast pace.

Within the multiple voices and in the course of its evolution, some patterns have emerged. I'll mention six of them. While my list is just that—*my list* of patterns that strike *me*—I think most persons would say it is true to the terrain.

Let me list the six basic patterns I see. Then I'll consider each one in turn.

1. an affirmation that *God hopes for human flourishing.*
2. a declaration that *theology is always political.*
3. an embrace of *incarnate experience as fundamentally trustworthy.*

—and because of these three claims—

4. a *rejection of authoritarian power in favor of relational power.*
5. a *commitment to the value of this world;*
6. and a *deep suspicion about any salvific role ascribed to suffering.*

The first claim, that God hopes for human flourishing, hardly seems controversial. But, as you'll see, when linked to the other claims it becomes a revolutionary assertion.

Politics, in its truest meaning, names the communal venture of organizing our life together. It may or may not have to do with political parties and elections; it may or may not have to do with formal models of government. But politics *inevitably* has to do with the patterns by which power is held, shared, transferred, and withheld among a group of people.

Often this notion of politics has simply been reduced to the endorsement of the status quo. It has meant little more than "the way we do things" or "the way God wants things done." But in the latter half of the twentieth century, GLBT persons, along with a whole array of marginalized persons have said, "No, wait. Politics is not divinely instituted, it is humanly chosen. It is up for debate. And for centuries it has been woefully misshapen by the monopoly on power that white straight men have claimed and have preserved for themselves."

And this imbalance in communal power has often been preserved with theological sanction. Our language about God inevitably shapes the way we view and value the world. And we have by and large imaged God as a white male, all-powerful and sexless. And so we have communities in which white men are the most privileged, and in which white male sexual appetites are merged—from movies to music to locker rooms—with the ideal of being all-powerful. Sex becomes conquest . . . and conquest becomes eroticized.

Hence, to say that theology is political is to say that power relations in any given community overlap with the way God is discussed, and it is to suggest that any legitimate discussion of the God who hopes for human flourishing—and not simply the flourishing of humans who happen to be white, or male, or straight—must include those voices traditionally silenced and dismissed. This leads to the third claim: that incarnate experience is fundamentally trustworthy.

The first step in securing the oppression of GLBT persons, the move that allows "us" to silence "their" voices and erase "their" lives, is the move that says, your experience of who you are is untrustworthy.

It is the message that most persons in the mainline churches get from their earliest days, but it troubles few persons as much as it does GLBT persons. I learned as a boy growing up that the Bible and the Church knew more about goodness than my own experience could convey, but because both church doctrine and biblical texts have been almost exclusively the work of straight men, their experience often included my own.

Persons of color and women have had a struggle similar to GLBT persons because they too have had to recognize that the sources of authority in the Christian tradition came out of experiences in which color and female-ness were noticeably absent. I won't argue here over which absence is most primal—they may well be interdependent—but the starting place for GLBT theology is here because until you can challenge the claim that dismisses the very life you live, you remain complicit in your oppression and have no foothold from which to challenge it.

The simple but strident claim is this: *"I matter. My life matters. My body matters. What I know, in my own experience, as deep joy matters. What I know, in my own experience, as betrayal and alienation matters."*

This is not to say that *all* experience is equally revelatory. It is not to say whatever feels good in the moment must be of God. But it is to say *because* God hopes for human flourishing (and any God who does not hope for this is not worthy of being God), and *because* theology is political (because it is always implicitly a discussion about who deserves power and how they will receive and hold it), *therefore my experience (because it is human) lies potentially within the hope of God and must be heard.*

From these three interwoven claims, three more follow.

First, a rejection of authoritarian power. Within GLBT theology there is a widespread affirmation that God is known in profound experiences of power shared in common with others, often referred to as "power-with" rather than "power-over."

This affirmation—grounded in experience—challenges a view in which God is seen as all-powerful and argues instead that God is all-relational. That God's "godness" is not a function of singular power but of universal presence.

It also calls into question the notion that Jesus—and Jesus alone—was God incarnate. Instead, much GLBT theology suggests that *all* humans have a capacity to manifest divine presence. Jesus did so with astonishing clarity, but to make his humanity uniquely divine supports an institutional structure in which clergy become his representatives and the holders of his delegated authoritarian power. In looking at the record of his lived life, GLBT persons see instead a clear practice of relational power, one which resonates with the moments of deep goodness in their own lives.

This rejection of authoritarian power also shapes the way that GLBT theologians approach the biblical text. It is, for most of them, still authoritative—it has a historical priority—but it is not authoritarian. It is a text of theology—of human talk about God—and as such it is political, and it is shaped by the power relations of the human community that produced it. Hence, it can—and must—be argued with whenever its words fail to reveal the God who longs for human flourishing.

And finally, this rejection of authoritarian power means that within GLBT theology the realm of sexual ethics is grounded not in hard and fast rules but in the honoring of relational integrity. There are perhaps few places where GLBT theology is more diverse than on questions of ethics, but overall I think it is fair to say that abusive power is rejected, safe vulnerability is prized, fidelity is measured by honesty and integrity, procreation is affirmed as the

160

care of creation in all its forms rather than merely the begetting of children, and sexual pleasure is claimed as one of God's best gifts.

How any particular relationship or behavior is assessed morally is not a matter of finding the right rule; it's a matter of looking carefully at the character of the relationship itself.

Second, the affirmation that bodily experience is potentially revelatory—rooted in the claim that embodiment is a gift from God—leads to a commitment to the value of *all* bodies and thus to the value of *this* world. GLBT theology recognizes that an unbalanced commitment to the *next* world has the predictable consequence of consoling those who hunger for justice *here* with the promise that they will get justice *there*—and thereby quietly condoning injustice here, since "here" is only a temporary place of relative value. Never mind that those who do the condoning often are the indirect beneficiaries of injustice in the meantime.

So GLBT theology, which may vary widely in its claims about the next world, is unstinting in its affirmation of the importance of this world. *Justice matters now.* And while that may begin in the recognition that they themselves are discriminated against, excluded, bashed, killed because of injustice, GLBT theology is increasingly vocal in claiming that justice is a seamless garment, that racial, gender, economic, and environmental justice are all essential aspects of human flourishing. At this point GLBT theology often goes "queer."

"Queer" has historically served as a term of contempt for GLBT persons. In its original meaning, queer means to "foul up," and to call a GLBT person queer was to say that they "fouled up" what it meant to be human. They spoiled the ideal. In recent years, GLBT persons have claimed this word as theirs to wield with pride. Not unlike the "black is beautiful" movement, to be queer and proud is to deny the oppressors symbolic use of language as a weapon against you.

But beyond this, when GLBT awareness, whether faith-based or not, becomes driven by a political vision that includes the flourishing of all, then to be "queer" is to actively seek to "foul up" the systems that perpetrate and perpetuate injustice. To be "queer" is to be subversive in a society where oppression is all too common on all too many fronts. To be "queer," in this

161

sense has less to do with one's bedroom activities than one's intentional work for justice in the wider world.

This leads me to the last pattern I want to highlight. When GLBT theologians look to Jesus they see someone who was supremely queer. In his healing on the Sabbath, his table-turning parables, his fellowship with women, his feasting with outcasts, they see a life determined to subvert the oppressive forces of society because of his vision of an all-welcoming God. And when they see this, it becomes clear to them that Jesus' death is not a sacrifice offered to God to pay the debt of human sin; it is the violent reaction of a society determined to maintain the status quo against the threat of grace. Hence, GLBT theology tends to downplay or outright reject the notion of a sacrificial death by Jesus. He was killed because he was queer, not because God needed innocent blood.

This theological move is also rooted in lived experience. When the dominant theology portrays a God willing to shed innocent blood through violence for the sake of redemption, it is all too easy for the institutional powers that claim to speak on behalf of God to decide where else blood must be shed to preserve that redemption. So infidels are massacred, pagan savages are slaughtered, witches are burned, Jews are marked for extermination, blacks are lynched, . . . and gays are bashed. Because GLBT persons have seen the theology of redemptive violence aimed at them, their own experience tells them this is a dangerous myth to entertain, and one that it is time for Christians (and others who hold it in different forms) to put to rest.

Well, that's a *whirlwind* tour of GLBT theology. It is amazing terrain, with many a nook and cranny we haven't even peeked at. I encourage all of you to visit there for yourselves.

As I conclude, it would be presumptuous of me, a Lutheran (a bit unorthodox, yes, but still a Lutheran) to imagine that I can tell you, either individually or as a Unitarian Church what this theology has to offer you. You can do that far better than I, and I hope my message this morning will inspire you to have the conversation for yourselves.

I will close by saying very simply what this theology has offered me.

It has echoed many of my own theological intuitions, and in so doing it has helped me further define and shape my own theological voice and the foundations of my own ethical discernment. I am not GLB or T, but I am queer—deeply committed to challenging oppression and creating justice.

It has reminded me that God speaks in many places—including some that have been marked "off limits" by church and society. This invites me to remember that the only limit to God's freedom is God's grace. *The last word uttered by God may well surprise us, but it will not fail to welcome us.*

And perhaps most personally, my sojourn with GLBT theology has encouraged me to listen with supreme care—and in the good company of others—to the echoes of truth in my own experience and in my own body. Without question both my spirituality and my sexuality are infinitely richer on this account. I have learned that in this inspired flesh, gifted by the presence of God in both my ache and my ecstasy, I am indeed at home. That is revelation, my friends. Where I come from we call it "Gospel"—news that is astonishingly good.

This is the first of several hymns I've written with clear messages of Christian welcome. This one was adopted by the Reconciling in Christ Program for use as its 2004 RIC Sunday Hymn of the Day. In it I try to remain true to much of the imagery in the original poetry of "Ode to Joy," while introducing welcoming imagery full force in the last two stanzas.

1. Word of Welcome
(June 2003)

In this holy place we gather, claimed through grace by God above;
Heaven's wings now wrap around us, downy depths of boundless love.
Freed from fears that keep us hidden, for the work that You desire.
Reconciling as we're bidden, hearts aflame with joyful fire.

Earth in all her verdant beauty sings Your joy made manifest;
Winged and finned and scaled and limbed life; fruitful frenzy, quiet rest.
Rushing wind and roiling waters, green of forest, blue of sky,
Dark of night and dawn of morning, all give praise to You on high.

As by imprint, nature offers witness to Your gracious care
So in freedom's faith we follow after Christ if we but dare.
Rushing wind of Spirit able, blowing from the most to least
From the font and for the table, born again and bid to feast.

Word of welcome walk among us, watching as these wineskins burst
Breaking bread and pouring wine for all who hunger, all who thirst.
Now as we go forth to scatter, may Your presence yet abide
Joy of life and Love of justice, be our Wisdom and our Guide.

Text: David R. Weiss, 2003
Tune: Beethoven, Ninth Symphony, Fourth Movement ("Ode to Joy")

Permission is given to photocopy Word of Welcome *for use in worship.*

I wrote this hymn for Maundy Thursday, but it would be appropriate to any service, particularly an evening one, where the Eucharist will be celebrated. I intentionally used the tune of a Christmas Carol . . . both to link Christmas to Holy Week/Easter, but also to emphasize the theme of incarnation as the driving power of Holy Week. This Eucharist is not about Jesus' impending death as a "necessary" or "destined" sacrifice, but about celebrating the life lived . . . and recognizing the impending death as the price exacted by worldly forces for that life . . . and about honoring that life not by remembering its sacrifice but by emulating its compassion.

2. It Was upon a Moonlit Night (Maundy Thursday)
(April 1, 2004)

It was upon a moonlit night/when Jesus broke the bread;
With friends now gathered at his side/in solemn voice he said,
"For, lo, these many days we have/proclaimed the Kingdom at hand;
In turns: at table, by tale, by touch/we've shown God gracious and grand.

"But now the forces of power and hate/make ready to bury this wheat,
Before their deeds are done, my friends/each of you, take and eat."
Then raising high the cup of wine/he looked the room around
And spoke once more of days now past/of children lost now found.

"My friends, the justice of our God/is sealed in gracious love;
As earth gives freely to the vine/so mercy flows above.
Yet 'gainst the mercy we freely shared/oppression has lengthened its reach.
And now, before my blood is spilled/from this cup, drink of you each."

With eyes aflame with fear and faith/did Christ thus finish the meal;
And we who gather at his request—rememb'ring, we render it real.
In mercy breaking the bread he gave/in kindness sharing the cup;
In love encount'ring the least of these/and thereby his wounds we bind up.

. . . In love encount'ring the least of these/and thereby raising Christ up.

Text: David R. Weiss, 2004
Tune: Richard S. Willis, Carol ("It Came Upon the Midnight Clear")

Permission is given to photocopy Moonlit Night *for use in worship.*

165

This is a choral hymn for Pentecost—waiting for choral music. The Council of Jerusalem (Acts 15) is when the early church decided that it had no right to impose circumcision on the Gentiles. I think this incident in the early church is the "teachable moment" in the current church discussion about homosexuality. Although the Council text does not seem to appear anywhere in the common lectionary, this would be a perfect hymn for Pentecost because the Council event—perhaps more than the rushing wind, fiery tongues, and multiple languages on Pentecost itself—demonstrates the church's willingness to be a People of the Spirit. The hymn (at least in my mind) has a chorus sung by a full choir with solo parts for Peter and Paul, a pair of verses for Peter and Paul to sing together, and a final verse repeated by the whole choir as a closing to the last chorus.

3. The Council of Jerusalem
(April 13, 2004)

Chorus:

    It was a glorious day in Jerusalem
    It was a glorious day in Jerusalem
    It was a glorious day in Jerusalem
    When Peter and Paul said to all of them:

    The kin-dom of God is wider, you see
    The family of God is fuller, you see
    The Spirit of God blows freer, you see
    Than ever we thought that it could be

Peter:

    I saw a blanket from heaven put down
    Forbidden foods set all around
    I said, "Dear Lord, what can it mean?"
    And God told me, "I call these clean!"

    When the call came next to please come preach
    As Cornelius and family did beseech
    I saw that the food was folks, you see
    Gentile—and yet clean as could be

    So I went and I preached right from my heart
    But don't you know—t'was merely the start
    Cause right then and there, came the wind
    God's Spirit eager to gather them in
    (Repeat Chorus)

166

Paul:

> I've traveled afar with Barnabas
> Won't you all please listen to us?
> We've seen the signs and wonders done
> By God whose reign exceeds the sun
>
> Isaiah of old had promised it true
> That God had gathering more to do
> In Gentile lands this is what we saw:
> The Spirit unlimited by the Law
>
> Where faith is sown in the human heart
> Nothing of ours can keep us apart
> From the love of God given as grace
> This is the truth we need to face
>
> (Repeat Chorus)

Peter and Paul:

> And who are we—or are any of you
> To tell the Lord what is proper to do?
> I know what the Word of the Lord has said
> But the Spirit of God is racing ahead!
>
> The gifts of God—the water and the word,
> The bread and the wine, and the heart well-stirred—
> Come to the church from heaven you see
> From the Spirit that blows mighty and free!
>
> (Repeat Chorus)

Then Final Chorus:

> The gifts of God—the water and the word,
> The bread and the wine, and the heart well-stirred—
> Come to the church from heaven you see
> From the Spirit that blows mighty and free!

Lacking music for "The Council of Jerusalem," I wrote a second Pentecost hymn in 2004, this time borrowing a familiar breezy tune. Here I suggest how the outpouring of the Spirit continues the work of God's welcome begun in Jesus' ministry, furthered in the welcome of the Gentiles, and ongoing still today. While not explicitly mentioning GLBT persons, you know that this is the welcome waiting in the wings.

4. Now the Welcome
(April 28, 2004)

Christ the healer, Christ the host, raising cup in festive toast
Christ the one who sets the feast, Christ the one who calls the least
Christ the holy, Christ the lowly, Christ the teller of new tales,
Christ the bearer of a God who never fails, never fails.

Thus the leper, thus the lame, alleluias both proclaim
Thus the deaf can hear a cry, thus the blind can use their eye
Thus the praying, thus the playing, thus the laughter and the grin
Thus the graciousness of God who gathers in, gathers in.

Then the Spirit, then the Friend, then the mighty Rushing Wind
Then the Wisdom from on high in the tongues of flame come nigh
Then the telling, then the yelling, then the hearing each their own
Then the wideness of God's love is thus made known, thus made known.

Then the blanket, then the food, Peter's palate by God wooed
Then the Spirit of the Lord on the Gentiles freely poured
Then the seeing and agreeing and the witness to the rest
Then the op'ning of the church at God's behest, God's behest.

Now the wonders, now the signs, mark of God's surprise designs
Now the mustard seed grown full, now the lamp atop the bowl
Now the thirsting, now the bursting, now the new wine spilling out
Now the welcome of our God hear us shout, hear us shout!

Text: David R. Weiss, 2004
Tune: Carl Schalk, Thine ("Thine the Amen, Thine the Praise")

Permission is given to photocopy Now the Welcome *for use in worship.*

This hymn, written for the extraordinary ordination of Jay Wiesner, uses the tune of the anthem of the Reformation to musically evoke the reformation still happening today. Jay's ordination text (John 7:38) involved water, so I changed the hymn's imagery from Fortress to River and borrowed a variety of watery biblical images to celebrate the event. Verse one echoes Amos 5:24 and Isaiah 44:3-4; verse two uses Psalm 1:3 and Isaiah 44:4; verse three employs Proverbs 9, Isaiah 55:1, Wisdom 7:27 and John 2:1-11; and verse four draws on John 7:38, Revelation 22:1, and Amos 5:24.

5. Our God's a River
(May 6, 2004)

Our God's a river of matchless might,/a cataract cascading
With justice full and foamy white,/and mercy never fading.
The desert sands shall sing,/as bursting forth a spring,
The barren rock will bloom,/and flowers break the gloom.
Our God will bring us new life.

Like trees that grow by flowing streams,/held sure by their deep-twined roots,
Our leaves unwithered by sunbeams,/our branches yielding fine fruits.
We'll not be moved by fear/for waters cool and clear
We have for finest drink/whate'er the rest may think.
Baptized, we are God's saplings.

As Wisdom bids us come to feast,/her table set with sweet fare
So come we all from great to least,/and joyful find our seat there
While water roils to wine,/and wheat bakes bread most fine
Her breath doth prophets swell/and friends of God as well.
So Wisdom builds Christ's body.

Festive organ interlude

Our hearts with living waters flow,/fed by God's river gleaming
From cloud on high to dew below,/and through our midst now streaming
Each stole we lay with zeal,/another wound will heal
See rushing justice roll,/God's church will be made whole
God's Spirit splashes o'er us!

Text: David Weiss, 2004
Tune: Martin Luther, Ein Feste Burg ("A Mighty Fortress")

Permission is given to photocopy Our God's a River *for use in worship.*

I wrote this hymn for Welcoming Sunday 2005 for the Reconciling in Christ Program. It echoes imagery from the assigned readings: Isaiah 9:2 "The people who walked in darkness have seen a great light . . ." and Matthew 4:23 which speaks of Jesus "proclaiming the good news of the kingdom." It reminds us that the kingdom was less a "message" than the very activity of Jesus' ministry itself—and that the heart of this activity was embodying the welcome of God. Hence, I shift "kingdom" to a non-patriarchal and non-hierarchical—and just plain more truthful "kin-dom." Though written with particular texts in mind, this hymn would be appropriate for any service in which the theme of God's welcome is central.

6. Shall We Hearken to the Kin-dom
(October 18, 2004)

Shall we hearken to the kin-dom, we who have in darkness trod?
There is light so brightly shining, leading to the home of God.

See the lame and leper leaping, hear the mute and deaf rejoice,
See the dead are merely sleeping, waking to his gospel voice.

See the blind regain their eyesight, see the outcast sit to feast,
Now the demons take to their flight, Jesus came to save the least.

Still the Kin-dom longs to widen, longs to welcome others home,
Holy Winds have yet to heighten, Spirit free to rush, to roam.

Refrain:

Yes, we'll hearken to the Kin-dom, the widening, the welcoming Kin-dom
Hearken with our lives to the Kin-dom that leads to the home of God.

Final refrain:

Yes, we'll hearken to the Kin-dom, the widening, the welcoming Kin-dom
Hearken with our lives to the Kin-dom that leads to the home of God.

As we hearken to the Kin-dom, the widening, the welcoming Kin-dom
Bearing in our very lives the Kin-dom, we become the home of God

Text: David R. Weiss, 2004
Tune: Robert Lowry, Hanson Place ("Shall We Gather at the River")

Permission is given to photocopy Shall We Hearken *for use in worship.*

In this new Christmas carol text set to a familiar Christmas carol tune I try to hint at the way Jesus' birth foreshadows the welcome that will mark his ministry—and to reveal the irony of his manger-birth by linking it to the meal by which we remember his death.

7. There's a Welcome in the Wooden (The Manger)
(December 1, 2004)

There's a welcome in the wooden out back of the inn,
A sweetness in swaddles like new-sewn wineskin,
And poorly strewn straw hints at ripe wheat rolled thin.
There's a welcome in the wooden out back of the inn.

See Mary, wrapped in wonder, this baby to bear,
The fruit of her womb with the world now to share.
And Joseph in shadows with fatherly care
Soon making their ready to flee Herod's snare.

Here shepherds, oft outcast, an unlikely sight,
Now guests of this prince by angelic invite.
And sand dunes sing silently deep in the night
As Magi move westward wooed on by starlight.

Here cattle and donkey, here sheep and goats, too,
Are beckoned as creatures, this child to view;
And angels in glory now offer their due.
This wooden speaks a welcome both wondrous and true.

Consider, with me, friends, this daring design:
A manger, made for feeding, a most hungry sign—
Already this infant, holds wheat and holds wine.
There's a welcome in the wooden that all come and dine.

And outside of the stable, those not yet called in,
Now come to the manger wherever you've been,
And hear, as the wooden will call you, too, kin.
There's a welcome in the wooden out back of the inn.

Text: David Weiss, Christmas 2004
Tune: Appalachian folk tune, adapted by John Jacob Niles, ("I Wonder as I Wander")

Permission is given to photocopy Welcome in the Wooden *for use in worship.*

171

I wrote this hymn, set to a tune found in the Renewing Worship Songbook, with the 2005 ELCA Churchwide Assembly in Orlando in mind. The theme of the Assembly is "Marked with the Cross of Christ Forever"; hence the use of that image here. Also, I draw on the image of "Goodsoil," the name taken by the Alliance groups working to promote full participation for GLBT people in the church. And I ironically invoke the image of "Solid Rock," the name taken by those opposing full participation, suggesting that ultimately even this solid rock will sing hosanna at Christ's coming.

8. We Are Your Soil
(June 3, 2005)

Who are we?—Lord, we are yours! We are marked forevermore
By the cross and by the word. In our hearts we've been stirred.
Darkness round us, still we sing; To the promise still we cling.
Waiting for the coming dawn; Solid rock turned to song.

We are good soil; we are your soil.
Sow your justice
In Christ's body still today!
Let compassion fill our lives, Lord.
Rocks and stones, now,
Sing hosanna to our God!

Who are we?—Lord, we are yours! We were baptized at the font,
Water splashing on our face, Marked forever by grace.
Gay and straight, we sing your praise. Bi and trans, our voices raise.
To the feast you bid us dine; Welcome bread, welcome wine.

We are good soil; we are your soil.
Sow your justice
In Christ's body still today!
Let compassion fill our lives, Lord.
Rocks and stones, now,
Sing hosanna to our God!

Text: David R. Weiss, 2005
Tune: Per Harling, Du är helig ("You are Holy")

Permission is given to photocopy We Are Your Soil *for use in worship.*

I wrote this hymn for Welcoming Sunday, January 2006. The lectionary texts (Jonah 3:1-5,10; 1 Corinthians 7:29-31; Mark 1:14-20) included a reading from Jonah (a prophet sent by God to preach to those "beyond our choices"—likely a fictional tale with the clear theme of declaring the wideness of God's love) as well as Mark's account of the call of the first disciples (telling of their immediate response and their readiness to join Jesus in gathering the kin of God).

9. O Christ Who Came
(October 14, 2005)

O Christ who came/through ancient prophet voices
Declaring hope/when hope was all but spent
Who offered life/to those beyond our choices,
Whose words beyond/our foolish wisdom went.
O Burning Bush/aflame for all creation,
Who bids us all/to turn aside and see;
O Christ who came/in hope that we might hasten
Your kin-dom come/and set your people free.

O Christ who came/to fisher-folk confounded
Yet left at once/their boats and nets behind
To join your work/of holy hope unbounded
Good news proclaim/and captives to unbind.
O Christ the Text/the Word of God brought to us
Who spread the feast/and beckoned all to dine;
O Christ who came/determined to renew us
Your kin-dom come/in water, bread, and wine.

O Christ who came/in rushing Wind of Spirit
In Pentecost/of welcome flaming bright
Unstop our ears/that we might finally hear it;
Soften our hearts/as well, restore our sight.
O Calling God/whose voice is never ending,
Whose hope is strong/whose Spirit yet does roam;
O Christ who *comes*/in all we are befriending
Your kin-dom come/your children welcome home.

. . . O Christ who comes/in welcome wide extending,
Now through our lives/invite your children home.

Text: David R. Weiss, 2005
Tune: Irish tune, arr. John Barnard, Londonderry Air ("O Christ the Same")

Permission is given to photocopy O Christ Who Came *for use in worship.*

173

This Lenten hymn reflects on what it means to say that we "stand in the shadow of the cross" and suggests that standing there means standing with those whose company Jesus kept.

10. In the Shadow of Your Cross
(March 20, 2006)

You first were laid in a manger
Cradled gently by wooden beams early
Their shadow playing in stable firelight.

You heard your mother sing sweetly
Her soul daily the Lord magnifying
Till her song came to life in your living.

You gathered all who would listen
Claiming mercy as God's holy yearning
And for this risking your name and your life.

You last were nailed to the timber
Hoisted roughly on wooden beams deadly
Such anger aimed at your love for the least.

We who have followed your footsteps
Making mercy the fruit of our living
When darkness threatens, Lord, steady our souls.

Refrain:

Sweet Lord, in the shadow of your cross
We are standing right here at your side
In the least of many sisters and brothers
We find you as we stand by their side.

Text: David R. Weiss, 2006
Tune: Cesáreo Gabaraín, Pescador de hombres ("You have come down to the lakeshore")

Permission is given to photocopy In the Shadow of Your Cross *for use in worship.*

I wrote this hymn for the 2ⁿᵈ Sunday of Easter (Thomas' need to touch Jesus). It lifts up a variety of images of touching Jesus: the woman with the flow of blood (Mark 5: 25-34); the woman at the well (John 4: 4-29); the anointing at Bethany (John 12:1-8); Mary Magdalene at the tomb on Easter morning (John 20: 1-18); Thomas' Easter encounter (John 20: 19-29). Verse 6 suggests that we, too, touch Jesus whenever we offer our healing touch to the wounds of the world today.

11. Touching Jesus
(April 8, 2006)

Precious Lord, in my need, many years did I bleed;
I reach out, and I touch—touch your hem.
I am healed, like the rest; lepers cleansed, children blest.
Touch your hem, precious Lord, make me whole!

By the well, as I drew, there to drink, I drank you.
I am down, I am out, I am naught.
But you stop, and you speak; you're the One whom we seek;
Our lives touch, precious Lord, and I'm whole!

At the edge, of the town, there I knelt, to the ground.
Pour the nard, wipe your feet, with my hair.
While you dine, on the bread, through my tears, see you dead
Precious Lord, fragrant love, in the air!

Easter morn, through my tears, call my name, bring me near,
And I hear, and I look, and I hope.
Over cross, over death, bringing life, drawing breath;
Precious Lord, once again, you are whole!

Easter Eve, I'm away; you were there, but I say,
Let me see, let me touch, let me know.
Once again, there you are; fingertips touch your scars;
In my heart, precious Lord, now I know!

Precious Lord, still your hands, bear your wounds, many lands:
Some are lost, some are least, some are hurt,
Let me touch you in deed, as I touch those in need;
Use my hands, Precious Lord, make them whole!

Text: David R. Weiss, 2006
Tune: Thomas A. Dorsey, Precious Lord ("Precious Lord, Take My Hand")

Permission is given to photocopy Touching Jesus *for use in worship.*

I wrote this hymn with the 2008 Lutherans Concerned/North America Assembly in mind; its chosen theme is "Hearts on Fire." The hymn sets the journey of GLBT Christians within the story of Emmaus and holds up, in particular, the issues of blessing committed relationships and ordaining GLBT persons in such relationships (which are the central GLBT issues facing the Evangelical Lutheran Church in America today.

12. Hearts on Fire
(December 23, 2006)

As if in the upper room, as if in God's holy womb
As we celebrate this meal, as God's welcome we reveal,
Hearts on fire, Christ's desire, that our faith be born anew,
And the kin-dom of our God be ever true, ever true.

Here we gather, glad we say, Christ is with us here today.
In the stories that we tell, hear the Holy Wind now swell.
Hearts on fire, soaring higher, comes the Dove on flaming tongue,
Dreams and visions for our old and for our young, for our young,

Once our people lived in fear, once our hope was hard to hear,
Once our lives were framed by fright, 'til that Pentecostal night.
Hearts on fire, holy choir, of a most surprising tune
In the Stonewall cries of pride that distant June, distant June.

From the alleys running scared, from the brutal hate laid bare,
To a sanctuaried space, to the claiming of our place.
Hearts on fire, we aspire, find our missing Body parts
And re-member—every member—whose we are, whose we are.

From the moment that we dare, ask another's life to share,
Mid the people gathered round, as our lives in love are bound.
Hearts on fire, steepled spires, tolling loud for lifelong love,
Witnessed by the church below and God above, God above.

Now the One who knows all needs, on good soil sows good seed,
From the ground some grain is lured, to the Table and the Word.
Hearts on fire, Christ's desire that this Body be made whole,
In the calling and the placing of the stole, of the stole.

Text: David R. Weiss, 2006
Tune: Carl Schalk, Thine ("Thine the Amen, Thine the Praise")

Permission is given to photocopy Hearts on Fire *for use in worship.*

I wrote this hymn as an antiphonal song: our voice is in the verses and God's response appears in the refrain. In it I place the present welcoming activity of churches into the larger biblical story of God's welcoming activity. Our work has its place because of God's voice in the refrain.

13. Behold, I Gather All to Me
(September 14, 2007)

Our song we sing in praise of God who swirled
Over chaos, hov'ring Wisdom, birthing the world.
Each word you spoke was so—and so was good.
Now, O Wisdom, on your Sabbath, sing if you would—

> Behold, I gather all to me; those I gather, I set free.
> Behold in me all things are new:
> At first light, and then in Christ, and now in you.

To slaves who cried to you from out their pain,
God of freedom, God of justice, in pow'r you came.
To gifts of law and land you led the weak,
Birthed a people, after your heart, who hear you speak—

And when your people sought to shut the door
'gainst the Gentiles, 'gainst the eunuchs, against the poor,
Then prophets spoke the passion of your choice
For the outcast—for the voiceless, they raised your voice—

> Behold, I gather all to me; those I gather, I set free.
> Behold in me all things are new:
> At first light, and then in Christ, and now in you.

In Christ your holy Wisdom dwelt on earth
Preaching welcome, bringing wholeness, and sharing mirth.
Though crucified, the resurrected One
Sends the Spirit, to God's people: the song goes on—

Our song we sing in praise of God today;
God who claims us, God who names us, both straight and gay.
And each is safely kept beneath your wing:
Loving holy, living fully, because you sing—

Behold, I gather all to me; those I gather, I set free.
Behold in me all things are new:
At first light, and then in Christ, and now in you.

Text: David R. Weiss, 2007
Tune: Traditional Peruvian, El Condor Pasa ("Flight of the Condor")

Permission is given to photocopy Behold, I Gather *for use in worship.*

Resources

How to order more copies of this book. The best way to get additional copies is to order direct through the book's website: **www.davidrweiss.com**.

Ordering direct from the book's website maximizes the income that actually gets back to the author—and increases the amount that becomes a donation to Wingspan Ministry. You can also order this book through your local bookstore or your preferred online bookseller.

A wide array of resources is available for GLBT persons of faith (and their allies). The handful that I identify here are simply a few select starting places. Each of these will be a gateway to many more.

Wingspan Ministry is a congregational ministry of St. Paul-Reformation Lutheran Church that provides pastoral care, education, advocacy and support for gay, lesbian, bisexual, and transgender people. Wingspan partnered in the publication of this book—and 25% of the book's profits are being donated to Wingspan. Wingspan helps St. Paul-Reformation Lutheran Church model a new way of being church that seeks to include all persons. The best way to experience the work of Wingspan is to join us for worship or fellowship activities at St. Paul-Reformation.

    Website: www.stpaulref.org
    Email: office@stpaulref.org
    Mail: 100 North Oxford Street, Saint Paul, MN 55104-6540
    Phone: 651-224-3371

Lutherans Concerned/North America works for the full inclusion of gay, lesbian, bisexual, and transgender Lutherans in all aspects of the life of their Church and congregations. I've worked in close partnership with LC/NA for several years. Their website will link you to a good number of other advocacy groups, both Lutheran and beyond.

    Website: www.lcna.org
    Email: admin@lcna.org
    Mail: PO Box 4707, Saint Paul, MN 55104-0707
    Phone: 651-665-0861

The Institute for Welcoming Resources, a program of the National Gay and Lesbian Task Force, is an ecumenical group that provides resources to facilitate a paradigm shift in multiple denominations so that churches become welcoming and affirming of all congregants regardless of sexual orientation and gender identity. They have a large set of resources and links to all their denominational partner organizations.

Website: www.welcomingresources.org
Email: info@WelcomingResources.org
Mail: 810 West 31ˢᵗ Street, Minneapolis, MN 55408
Phone: 612-821-4397

Soulforce is a national organization that pursues freedom for gay, lesbian, bisexual, and transgender people from religious and political oppression through the practice of relentless nonviolent resistance. They frequently work with denominational advocacy groups to strategize ways to use active nonviolence both to garner media attention and to transform hearts.

Website: www.soulforce.org
Email: info@soulforce.org
Mail: PO Box 3195, Lynchburg, VA 24503

The Catholic Pastoral Committee on Sexual Minorities is a grassroots, self-supporting, and independent coalition dedicated to promoting ministry to, with, and on behalf of GLBT persons—primarily of a Roman Catholic background—and their families and friends. This progressive Catholic group seeks to help GLBT Catholics integrate their sexual identities with their faith heritage.

Website: www.cpcsm.org
Email: cpcsm@ourtownusa.net
Mail: 2930 13th Avenue South, Minneapolis, MN 55407-1420
Phone: 612-201-4534

The Naming Project seeks to provide a safe and sacred space where youth of all sexual orientations and gender identities know themselves to be named and claimed by a loving God. Through its unique summer camp program, youth are able to explore and share their faith, experience healthy and life-giving community, reach out to others, and advocate for systemic change in church and society.

Website: www.thenamingproject.org
Email: staff@thenamingproject.org.
Mail: 2511 East Franklin Avenue, Minneapolis, MN 55406